Teaching Primary English through Drama

Teaching Primary English through Drama builds on the success of the classic text *Drama in Primary English Teaching*, inspiring ideas and techniques for teaching English skills through the medium of drama.

Focusing on the power of drama to promote effective learning in primary education, Suzi Clipson-Boyles demonstrates how reading, writing, speaking and listening skills may be developed in ways that will motivate and engage pupils. She uses specific examples from the English curriculum, and also makes links to other areas of the curriculum. The book explains how assessment during drama can help teachers to evaluate pupils' progress in English. Further guidance is given on how drama can enrich studying for pupils who are learning English as a foreign language. The book also provides a chapter on developing drama as an art form in its own right, with simple ideas and practical suggestions on how to enhance performances.

Teaching Primary English through Drama presents a wide range of drama approaches from ten-minute starter activities to stimulate ideas, such as fun ways to practise reading, through to longer projects that can provide contexts for extended writing or help with presentation and performance. The chapters show how drama can help to bring lessons alive in imaginative ways that not only promote enjoyment but also enhance achievement.

This comprehensive and practical guide offers essential reading for primary teachers and other practitioners, and is a valuable resource to trainees. It also provides an excellent foundation for those who wish to extend their expertise further towards drama as a subject specialism.

Suzi Clipson-Boyles is a national leader in school improvement. She has over 30 years' experience as a teacher, head teacher, teacher trainer, local authority adviser and Her Majesty's Inspector (HMI). Her previous publications include *Drama in Primary English Teaching*, *Supporting Language and Literacy 0–5* and *Putting Research into Practice in Primary Teaching and Learning*, all published by David Fulton.

Teaching Primary English through Drama

A practical and creative approach

Second edition

Suzi Clipson-Boyles

Routledge
Taylor & Francis Group

LONDON AND NEW YORK

KH

First published as *Drama in Primary English Teaching* 1998
By David Fulton Publishers

This edition published 2012
by Routledge
2 Park Square, Milton Park, Abingdon, Oxon OX14 4RN

Simultaneously published in the USA and Canada
by Routledge
711 Third Avenue, New York, NY 10017

Routledge is an imprint of the Taylor & Francis Group, an informa business

British Library Cataloguing in Publication Data
A catalogue record for this book is available from the British Library

Library of Congress Cataloging in Publication Data
Clipson-Boyles, Suzi.
Teaching primary English through drama : a practical and creative approach / by Suzi Clipson-Boyles. — 2nd ed.
p. cm.
Prev. pub. as: Drama in primary English teaching / Suzi Clipson-Boyles.
Includes bibliographical references and index.
1. English language — Study and teaching (Elementary) — Great Britain.
2. Drama in education — Great Britain. I. Clipson-Boyles, Suzi. Drama in primary English teaching. II. Title.
LB1576.C5655 1998
372.6'044–dc22
2011004189

ISBN: 978-0-415-59691-6 (hbk)
ISBN: 978-0-415-59692-3 (pbk)
ISBN: 978-0-203-81738-4 (ebk)

Typeset in Bembo and Helvetica Neue LT Pro
by Prepress Projects Ltd, Perth, UK

MIX
Paper from
responsible sources
FSC
www.fsc.org   FSC® C004839

Printed and bound in Great Britain by
TJ International Ltd, Padstow, Cornwall

2/28/12

Contents

Illustrations

Acknowledgements

Thank you very much to Laura and Daisy for allowing me to reproduce their personal writing, and also to Alana for her contribution. And finally thank you to all my many former pupils who have inspired me with their ideas and creativity, and have repeatedly proved to me over the years that drama is a truly wonderful and effective way to learn!

Preface

This book has been written especially for primary teachers and trainees who wish to introduce drama into their classroom practice as a means of teaching English skills. It not only covers the obvious requirements for drama within the English curriculum, but also describes how drama techniques can be used to teach other English skills. It sets the context by providing a short background to drama in primary education and explaining the strong learning links between drama and English.

It provides the basic components of drama teaching, including the wide range of techniques available and how to organise and manage your classroom when teaching drama. It then goes on to discuss oracy, reading and writing in individual chapters to enable you to examine specific potential for learning in each area in more depth, and to assist easy reference. However, it is important to remember that in reality these components of English are inextricably linked. An integrated approach to English, in which oracy, reading and writing are part of a complex linguistic inter-relationship, is at the heart of all good practice when teaching language. That is the nature of primary education at its best. In order to make explicit this integration, examples of drama activities are provided throughout and there is useful cross-referencing between chapters. Supporting the development of language and literacy skills is explained further in a chapter on supporting children for whom English is an additional language.

Drama can also operate as a discrete art form in the curriculum, and again there is inevitable overlap between content and skills from other areas, particularly English. However, additional guidance is provided in a chapter on theatre and performing arts for those who wish to extend their drama further towards this specialism. The book finishes with a chapter on assessment which includes a simple framework for monitoring and planning the progression of drama in English.

The book emphasises throughout that there are many approaches to drama, and different time-scales from five minutes upwards, depending on the purpose of the activity. For those who are new to teaching drama, it is advisable to introduce activities into your practice gradually – in bite-size chunks! Start with something that feels comfortable to you, where you will feel firmly in control and which has clear learning objectives. The results will almost certainly inspire you to try more!

Suzi Clipson-Boyles

2011

Making time for drama

Chapter overview

This chapter aims to help you understand how and why drama can add value to your teaching of English. It discusses:

- the time pressures of teaching English

- the emergence of drama in primary education

- the effectiveness of drama for learning

- developing a whole-school approach to drama.

The time pressures of teaching English

Raising standards in English has always been the top priority on government agendas across the years. Similarly, most parents and carers measure the success of a school by how well their child can read and write. As a result, increasing amounts of time have been spent on teaching literacy, sometimes at the expense of other areas of the curriculum, including speaking and listening. Teachers can therefore perhaps be forgiven for worrying that they do not have enough time to fit in drama! And yet, despite intensive and relentless drives to spend more time on literacy in primary schools, standards have barely risen. In particular, the quality of children's writing remains a concern. The reality is that many hours can be wasted when children are given inappropriate tasks that are of no interest, have no meaningful context and do not move the learning forward at a sufficiently rapid pace.

Good English teaching is not just about *what* is taught, but also about *how* it is taught. Children need to learn, practise and rehearse literacy and oracy skills in a wide range of relevant contexts if they are to engage with what they are learning and make good progress. The challenge for teachers is to make that process interesting, interactive and sufficiently challenging. Drama is one approach that teachers can adopt to provide such opportunities, and it is an extremely effective tool. Including drama in your planning can add significant value to your teaching, and should be regarded as an integrated part of English teaching rather than an additional requirement and pressure on time. There is a wide choice of drama approaches that can be used to help children to learn, practise and apply the basic skills of reading, writing, speaking and listening. These range from five-minute starters to stimulate ideas through to more sustained performance or presentation of work for an audience. The different ways of working along this spectrum are described in more detail in Chapters 2 and 3, and practical examples of how these can be used to teach English are provided throughout the book. However, before going into the finer detail of practical application, let us look first at the wider place of drama in primary education, and how it has reached the point that it is at today.

The emergence of drama in primary education

Finding a useful definition for primary drama has often been difficult because views have sometimes been polarised by different pedagogical debates. On the one hand, there are those who believe that drama is a pure art form, directly aligned with creative expression, theatre and performance. The purists in this camp dislike the notion of drama being used as a 'vehicle' for teaching other subjects, seeing such an approach as a dilution of the art form and an erosion of its status. At the other extreme, there are those who regard drama as a process of self-exploration and development – a means by which children can interact (rather than act) during simulated or improvised experiences provided to assist their learning. The purists in this camp dislike any notion of theatricality, rehearsal or performance.

There is also a middle ground in the case of primary drama that is not a watering down of both views at the halfway point, but rather a relationship between the two, within which there is a choice of different approaches. These all have different but equally valuable contributions to make to good-quality primary education, from experimental writing in the role-play area through to sophisticated reinterpretations and presentation of work from Shakespeare. This is a useful, balanced and educationally appropriate model for use in primary schools that can address the learning needs of young children, and the practicalities of fulfilling those needs for a class of 35 as part of a packed curriculum! In order to help you understand how this rich and varied model of drama has developed, let us first look at the emergence of drama in the primary school during the last 70 years.

The 1944 Education Act represented a determination to provide children with a new kind of education that would develop them in a more balanced and holistic way. Freedom and self-expression were of critical importance to a nation that was recovering from the repression of two world wars. The arts were to play an important role in this revolutionary approach to education that had never been seen before in Britain.

In the 1950s, drama in education took a further turn of direction as the focus moved away from the 'performance approach' and instead prioritised the experiential elements of child drama. In other words, rather than the more traditional rehearsing and polishing traditional work to present to an audience, children were provided with opportunities to play with ideas and experience situations as a means of gaining insight into and understanding of different themes. The work of Peter Slade (1958) was instrumental in developing these new developmental and experiential approaches. It can be no coincidence that this innovative work was taking place during the same decade as the work of child development theorists such as Piaget (1952), whose research was highlighting the links among interaction, speech, thought and learning development.

This exploratory approach to drama in education continued into the 1960s and 1970s as more and more proponents of the method emerged. Brian Way (1967) was a key figure in providing useful practical guidance for teachers, as was Gavin Bolton (1979) during the next 10 years. The high profile of experiential educational drama culminated in the legendary work of Dorothy Heathcote (see Wagner, 1999), and the impact of her work remains influential to this day. Her work demonstrated astounding results with children nationally: more in-depth learning; improved understanding; effective organisation of ideas; alternative expressions and presentations of those ideas; and high levels of engagement and enjoyment of learning. By this time, drama featured significantly in primary education and was included prominently in teacher training courses, as its value to children's learning and development was widely recognised. This belief went from strength to strength and survived well into the 1980s. However, concerns started to emerge about the lack of depth and rigour in the primary curriculum. Gaps were identified in children's knowledge and skills, particularly in English and mathematics, and the 1988 Education Act introduced a statutory National Curriculum to address these problems.

For the next 20 years, drama in primary education underwent major changes and challenges. Despite the fact that short references to drama were made within the different strands in the Orders for English (DES, 1989), it was now largely forgotten about by schools because of the time pressures of an extremely full and prescriptive curriculum, and this period marked the start of a decline. Educational drama was reduced from a rich and thriving part of primary education to a virtually extinct area of learning. Drama's hidden place within English plus brief references to it as a teaching approach in the Orders for mathematics, history, geography and science were not sufficient for schools to see it as mainstream. The significant reduction of drama on initial teacher training courses also meant that expertise in schools was slowly but surely disappearing.

Concerns were raised at various points along the way. In 1990, Her Majesty's Inspectorate of Education (HMI) published a report on the teaching and learning of drama in primary schools. This endorsed the educational value of drama. 'The most successful work in primary schools . . . shows that drama not only has value as a vehicle for work in other subjects; it is also important in its own right and is widely appealing to primary children' (HMI, 1990: page 5, paragraph 3). In 1991, the National Curriculum Council produced a poster entitled *Drama in the National Curriculum*, offering guidance to teachers on ways in which they could use drama to teach across the curriculum (NCC, 1991). The Arts Council England also responded to the omission of drama as a foundation subject by producing its own programmes of study for schools to follow in a full report entitled *Drama in Schools* (Arts Council England, 1992). In addition to recommending the inclusion of drama as an arts subject, the report highlighted the valuable part that drama could play in children's learning: 'Drama can contribute powerfully to the quality of learning in many areas of the primary school curriculum' (page 1, paragraph 1.4).

Despite these determined professional attempts by well-respected sectors of the education world to persuade teachers to include drama in their regular planning, the tide of curriculum content had swept over the land of pedagogy and psychology of how young children learn. A hefty, one-size-fits-all delivery model for English became the norm in most schools. The introduction of the National Literacy Strategy Teaching Framework (DfEE, 1998) was the final nail in drama's coffin, despite sparse references to strands of drama related to speaking and listening. During the final decade of the twentieth century, the tightly structured government approach to teaching English in primary schools left little room for creativity by pupils or teachers, and drama all but disappeared from most primary schools.

In 1999, the revised National Curriculum included drama as a more specific strand within the English requirements for speaking and listening (see Chapter 4). The specifics were included under a drama sub-heading, which raised the profile marginally. In 2003, the Qualifications and Curriculum Authority (QCA) sent to all schools a pack of new materials to support the teaching of speaking and listening, including drama. This was in response to growing concerns that the impoverished oral skills of an increasing number of children were having a negative impact on their literacy development. It was also in recognition of the fact that the teaching of speaking and listening was being neglected in many schools.

In 2003, the Arts Council England produced a second edition of its publication *Drama in Schools*, demonstrating that the original still provided very useful guidance for schools but needed updating. It was optimistic about the state of drama in secondary schools, but provided little convincing evidence that drama in the primary sector was alive and well. However, useful case studies of good practice in the (then) Foundation Stage, Key Stage (KS) 1 and Key Stage 2 were provided, along with useful programmes of study. Eight years later, at the time of writing this book, *Drama in Schools* remains the only substantial national framework for teaching drama in primary schools. It also provides a clear and compelling argument that drama can make an important contribution to children's wider development – the effectiveness of drama for learning.

The effectiveness of drama for learning

Drama is an art form that is a vital part of our heritage. In primary education, it can also travel beyond this in terms of children's learning, and there should be no doubt in any teacher's mind that there are compelling reasons to include drama in the primary curriculum. The four main reasons for this are:

- drama is a powerful vehicle for contextualising and using language
- it assists learning, understanding and memory through active engagement and experience
- it is an effective medium for expressing and communicating thoughts and ideas

- it is an important part of our artistic and cultural heritage.

Let us consider each of these roles in more detail.

Drama and language

Language lies at the core of human communication and learning. Literacy and oracy are high-priority areas in the National Curriculum. They also support children's learning in other subjects because the curriculum, particularly at Key Stage 2, is designed with the assumption that children can read, write, listen to instruction and talk about their work. Drama puts language into action in ways that children can identify with, respond to and learn from. It brings language alive by providing meaningful contexts. These include roles, purposes and audiences, all of which give the language authenticity in the eyes of the children.

Drama and learning

Drama assists the learning process by enabling children to engage actively with their subject matter. In the role-play area, children play out the roles of characters and encounter situations from new perspectives. Their responses can reshape their thinking because the process of active engagement and externalisation of thought are contributing to the ways in which things become organised in their minds. Older children taking part in the simulation of a Viking funeral will be applying their existing knowledge to the situation, acquiring new knowledge and theories from the actions of others, and developing new thoughts and responses in ways which would never arise from simply listening to an account. There is much evidence to support the hypothesis that all these things will also be retained more efficiently in the long-term memory because of the interactive nature of the learning process.

Drama for expressing and communicating

Children produce work in a variety of formats in school: topic books, writing for displays, fiction, reports, newspapers, paintings and so on. Drama offers yet another medium for the expression and presentation of learning. There are different ways this can happen, as you will see as you continue to read this book. It might be a group of five children displaying freeze-frame pictures of Aztec scenes after researching this from non-fiction books or the Internet; it might be a puppet play performance of *Macbeth*, or it could be an in-role presentation of why a new motorway should or should not be built. As with any piece of work, these end-products should be created with high expectations of children's preparation, organisation and communication. Standards should be high. Assessment and recording of the learning taking place should also be part of this process, and this is discussed in Chapter 10.

Drama as an art form

Drama is a universal cultural phenomenon, crossing geographical boundaries as it emerges in many forms around the world. Likewise, it goes back through history – the word 'drama' is derived from Ancient Greek (meaning 'action') – the literature of and approaches to theatre through the ages are well documented. Although *theatre* takes on many styles and genres, even within different cultures, the drama is the unifying element that is at the heart of them all. The power of story, the transmission of knowledge, the shaping of ideas and emotions into an art form that is alive, dynamic and interactive, all make connections with human response to resonate with life itself! It is part of our heritage, it is part of the communication and transmission of ideas and thought, and all children should have equal opportunities to enjoy it, learn about it, use it and be enriched by it. This will happen only if it is firmly embedded as a requirement within our educational system.

Applying the four rules

Table 1.1 below provides some examples to demonstrate how drama might be used in each of these four ways. This matrix is a simple overview to help you to start thinking about the different ways in which drama can be used. You will also note here that each drama category offers scope for integration with the others.

It is important to consider this vital issue of integration, even though the four primary categories of focus are separated here for the purpose of identification and explanation. For example: oracy skills would be developed during the debate in geography, the Greek puppet play could sit appropriately within a topic on Ancient Greece, and the simulation of a Victorian workhouse might eventually lead to a presentation. Nevertheless, it is useful to be aware of these four categories if you are to build a sound professional understanding of the workings and potential of drama.

The benefits described here speak for themselves, and there will be teachers out there who need no convincing. However, the real long-term benefits to a child are best reaped in schools where there is a consistent approach to drama from Reception to Year 6. In the absence of a statutory developmental framework it is up to schools, and in particular headteachers, to ensure that children follow a progressive continuum as they move through primary school – starting in the Early Years Foundation Stage with stories and natural and imaginative role-play, and gradually moving on to use the conventions and communication tools of theatre arts. For this to happen most effectively, an agreed whole-school approach is required.

TABLE 1.1 Examples of the four roles of drama in the primary curriculum

LANGUAGE[a]	LEARNING	COMMUNICATING	ART FORM
Oracy: using specific type of speaking in role **Reading:** interpreting scripts **Writing:** recording an interview in role	**Art:** exploring feelings and moods after drama **Geography:** in-role exploration of environmental issues **History:** simulation of Victorian children in the workhouse	**Science:** reporting the weather in role **PSHE:** presenting the impact of bullying as a documentary **RE:** presenting aspects of festivals	Presentation of Shakespeare Dance-drama to portray the water-cycle Presentation of a Greek play by puppets

a See Chapter 10, pages 129–30, for examples of how these might be differentiated.

Planning a whole-school approach to drama

Introducing drama across the whole school is challenging, particularly when staff lack confidence about their abilities to teach drama. Planning a school's approach together as a team has many benefits. You can ensure that coverage is developmental and varied to suit the needs of the children at each stage. This also adds strength to what you are building because the children will be accumulating skills and knowledge as they move through the school that will underpin other new approaches as they are introduced. Team planning provides mutual support, where ideas can be shared and discussed and suggestions offered. But, perhaps most importantly, staff who work together in a holistic way with agreed aims, commitment and enthusiasm can have an astounding impact on the quality of the learning. Confident individual teachers might well offer a memorable year of drama to their own class, but the value of that learning will be the proverbial drop in the ocean! In comparison, seven years of progressive drama education during which children are developing competencies in a targeted range of skills is more likely to produce confident and creative learners with a good knowledge of theatre arts and a sense of ownership and control of language and drama as an expressive form. Such planning ideally needs to be coordinated by a designated drama leader.

The role of the curriculum leader

Headteachers who facilitate the role of curriculum leader for drama are acknowledging the value and effectiveness of drama as a teaching tool, the impact it can have upon children's learning, the integral place of drama within language and literacy, and the cultural and social value of theatre arts in education. The role of the drama leader is to work with the staff to ensure that a comprehensive and successful drama programme operates from the Early Years Foundation Stage through to Year 6. Responsibilities might include the following:

- keeping well informed as an 'expert' through journals, websites, books and courses
- disseminating this information to staff
- providing professional development for staff
- inducting new staff into the school drama approach
- modelling good practice
- coordinating a comprehensive programme of theatre visits
- arranging visits by professionals to school
- coordinating seasonal events and maximising their potential for learning (e.g. Christmas performances)
- building up a collection of useful resources (e.g. play scripts, costumes, sound effects CDs)
- organising extra-curricular drama (e.g. trips, workshops, productions)
- organising theatre trips for staff, parents or carers, and governors.

Sensitivity to staff needs and attitudes is a significant feature of this role. A flamboyant, extrovert drama teacher may inspire, but can also frighten other members of staff who feel less confident! It is important to be a good listener, and empathise with those who feel unsure about teaching drama. Encouraging staff to try out ideas in bite-size chunks is more likely to work than forcing them before they are ready.

Assessment and record keeping

Efficient ways of recording assessments and linking these to planning can ensure better overall achievement because they enable each teacher to build more accurately on children's strengths as they move up through the school. On the other hand, too much unnecessary paperwork can create a barrier to children's progress by taking valuable time away from teachers, so record keeping should be realistic, useful and manageable. The assessment model provided in Chapter 10 relates specifically to drama as part of the National Curriculum requirements for English and shows how planning can be differentiated.

Theatre visits

The ideal expectation is that every child should experience live theatre every term. This would very likely include trips out as well as visiting performers coming into school. The range of responses to the work of others which the National Curriculum requires cannot be developed fully from only one visit every couple of years. Children need to develop the 'theatre habit' and become confident critics. An annual visit for each class should be the absolute minimum.

Cost is a problem only if we allow it to remain a problem! Many parents and carers are delighted that schools will take their children to the theatre, and we should not assume that they will be unwilling to pay. We should, however, do our very best to ensure that parents and carers understand the benefits of theatre visits, so that they appreciate the valuable learning rather than seeing it purely as leisure. Clearly, not all parents and carers *are* able to pay. An open pricing policy works in some schools (pay what you can afford). This needs subsidy, and the size of that subsidy will depend very much on the economic catchment area of the school. Some approaches to funding subsidies are:

- use of ongoing parent–teacher association funds
- dedicated fundraising event once a year (e.g. The Theatre Fund Raffle)
- business sponsorship
- Arts Council funding
- Lottery funding.

It can also be helpful to some parents and carers to offer a 'savings bank', to which the children can contribute a small sum each week. Appendix 4 includes a theatre visits log sheet which you might like to use as a record of the performances each child sees as he or she moves through the school. There are also four photocopiable theatre visit review sheets for different ages and/or abilities.

Whole-school awareness of the 'drama toolbox'

Facilitating and modelling good practice is one of the most important of the roles listed earlier for the curriculum leader for drama. A whole-school approach to delivering an effective drama curriculum for English requires teachers to use the full range of drama tools at appropriate points. Drama consists of many different approaches for different purposes, and the next chapter now goes on to explain the most effective of these with some practical examples.

Getting to know the tools of drama

Chapter overview

This chapter aims to equip you with a variety of approaches to drama that can be used for learning across the English curriculum. It begins by discussing:

- the range of drama techniques for learning

- the difference between experience and performance

- the importance of linking method to purpose

- differentiating the learning.

It then goes on to describe 23 drama techniques with practical cross-curricular examples, and ends with a chart showing where each one can be used for learning different English skills.

The range of drama techniques for learning

Just as a carpenter needs different tools for different tasks, a teacher needs different pedagogical tools to facilitate a range of learning experiences for children. Drama is not just one tool; it is a toolbox full of effective approaches to teaching and learning. Some teachers have been known to worry that drama is a high-risk, unstructured and sometimes noisy activity that requires hall time with the whole class. Not true! Others sometimes think that drama is about training children to act. Again, this is not the case, but both these misconceptions can occasionally mean that those teachers avoid drama because they do not have enough allocated time in the hall, they feel afraid they may lose control of the class, or they do not feel they have enough specialist knowledge. This chapter outlines simple drama techniques that can be developed one by one and eventually become an everyday part of your teaching tool kit!

There is no such thing as a typical drama lesson. Instead there is a wide and wonderful range of possibilities from which you can pick and mix according to the required learning intentions. It is also important to understand that drama does not have to be a whole-class activity in a large space, nor does it necessarily require an extended period of time. There are choices to make about how you organise the drama: from pairs to whole class; from sitting at a desk to moving around a hall; from five minutes to a three-week project. These aspects of planning and organisation are explained more fully in Chapter 3. Perhaps more importantly, there are choices you can make about the drama method you use. One useful way of defining each method is to consider whether it is simply going to be a vehicle for the children to experience or explore a theme or it is a means of performing their work. In some cases it might be a combination of the two. Let us look at the differences between experience and performance in order to better understand the choices.

The difference between experience and performance

Chapter 1 explained the emphasis on experiential child drama during the 1970s and 1980s, rather than the performance of school plays. The main difference between the two is that experiential work is usually not repeated, whereas performance is planned, shaped, rehearsed and ultimately presented to others. There is a place for both in primary schools. Sometimes it will be useful to move the learning process towards the performance end of the spectrum and sometimes it will not. For example: having explored or researched a theme in improvisation, children might go on to present their five-minute ideas to the rest of the class; the performance of a more structured collation of a project might be shown to the rest of the school in an assembly; or an even larger-scale production might be presented to a more public audience. Where meaningful contexts are provided and the children are fully involved in the planning, design and delivery of a performance, there is much learning that can take place from working on the production of a theatrical performance. This can cover a broad range of skills and knowledge right across the curriculum and is discussed in more detail in Chapter 9. However, sometimes it will be sufficient to explore ideas through the drama but not present them at all. For example: role-play in pairs might be a means of generating ideas for a piece of writing. Drama in the primary curriculum is about experience, reflecting on that experience, and sometimes, if relevant to the learning, performing in order to communicate the experience. The two extremities of the spectrum are only described here for the purposes of defining purpose more sharply. In reality, there is a whole range of options from which you can select that lie all the way along the spectrum from one end to the other. These can be used as a 'one-off' (e.g. conscience alley might be used to develop an analysis of character motivation) or might be linked together (e.g. following up the ideas generated during conscience alley with script writing for eventual performance of the character battling with their thoughts). The crucial point to be made here is that a drama technique should be selected appropriately according to the learning that needs to take place: in other words, linking method to purpose.

The importance of linking method to purpose

Good planning for your children's learning in any area of the curriculum should start with the following questions.

- What do they know already and how does this differ between ability groups?[1]
- What do they need to learn next and how can my planning differentiate the learning?
- What experience or activity can I provide to help them learn those things effectively, and with enjoyment and engagement?

Different drama techniques offer different opportunities for learning so there will be many reasons for including drama in your planning. We have already established that there is a range of tools from which to choose. It is therefore important to be discerning when making choices about method according to how it will contribute to the quality of the learning. The obvious starting point is what will be best for the children. What will the children take from the experience? How will it help them learn? How will it feel from their point of view? Will it provide the necessary focus, information, time and opportunities for them to learn, practise or consolidate the intended skills, knowledge or understanding? Here are some examples of matching approach to purpose:

mime	⟷ to assist memory by miming and guessing
tableaux	⟷ to provide a format for the presentation of research
dynamic duos	⟷ to practise particular forms of speech
script reading	⟷ to practise reading with expression and fluency
writing in role	⟷ to stimulate ideas while writing for a purpose
dance-drama	⟷ to provide an art form for the exploration of emotions in a poem.

Differentiating the learning

The examples provided in the next section are not full lesson plans, but are intended to give an overview of drama techniques in action. A full lesson plan should take into account the learning needs of different ability groups. For example, although the whole class may be writing in role, the learning objective for the actual writing is likely to differ between groups: some may be concentrating on using full stops and capital letters correctly, whereas others might be developing an understanding of how to organise their material into sequential paragraphs. More guidance is given on differentiation in Chapter 10.

Techniques for drama

The 23 effective drama techniques that follow are listed mostly in alphabetical order. Many can be used either experientially, as an expressive form, or both. Each one is explained in simple form and practical examples given for Key Stages 1 and 2. At the

---

1 Differentiation is the art of linking planned learning to formal and informal assessments of what the children already know. What they know already will usually span different levels.

end of the chapter, Table 2.1 shows where each technique can be used as part of learning across the four strands of English.

1: Conscience alley

This is a short technique to be used with a class when learning about or considering opposing views, in particular when a decision has to be made. The aim is to provide conflicting commentaries to be presented from both sides of an 'alley' of people. One person experiences the simultaneous sounds of the voices as they walk slowly down the alley. When they get to the end, they have to decide which side convinced them the most and make their choice. The value is not just in the experience for the walker but also in the planning by the children forming the alley. Each group should discuss and prepare words, phrases, questions, challenges and so on according to the focus. There is scope for exploring intonation, volume and expression as they plan and practise how they will say their words and phrases. Research can be a further extension, depending on the subject matter. Conscience alley should be treated with caution, especially if dealing with particularly emotive issues, bullying for example. It can be a powerful experience to walk through, and is considered less suitable for younger children. Always check that a child is feeling all right and back to normal after participating as the walker – they may need to talk about the experience.

(KS1) EXAMPLE

Not appropriate for younger children

(KS2) EXAMPLE   **An eye for an eye**

Time: 15 minutes

After being picked on in the playground, a child is deciding whether to get their revenge on the perpetrator by stealing their mobile phone from their bag in the cloakroom. The children prepare the arguments for and against.

2: Dance-drama

Exploring and presenting themes or stories through music and movement can be an exciting and powerful way for children to work. Remember that they will need a lot of preparation work first. Exploring ideas, experimenting with movement and shape, and expressing responses to music will all contribute to shaping a piece so that it tells a story. The value to English can be in the discussion and planning. Narratives might also be added if appropriate, providing opportunities for writing and reading aloud.

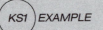 EXAMPLE   **The exploding machine**

Time: 15 minutes

Having built a machine of moving parts, where every child is a component and many components are connected in interesting ways, what happens to the machine if the speed is turned up too high and there is an explosion? Slow motion, use of levels, twisting, changing direction if they collide with another moving part etc.

 EXAMPLE   **The bully**

Time: 10 minutes whole-class discussion/20 minutes group work/15 minutes sharing

Read poem 'Duncan Gets Expelled' by Jackie Kay (1994). Discuss bullying and racism. Why? Who? Feelings? Solutions? In groups, the children create a movement piece to express mood and feeling. It can tell a story, but doesn't need to. Select powerful music for this with a strong beat.

3: Detached voices

In this approach one child speaks while another child performs the actions of the same character. The voice might be behind a screen or shadowing the body. This can also be used to express the thoughts of a character. Animal characters are very popular with young children, and this method is particularly effective for children who are reluctant to speak.

 EXAMPLE   **Puppet plays**

Time: 10 minutes planning/5 minutes performance

Having chosen characters from a story and made lollipop stick puppets, the children take turns showing the story to the class, with some children operating puppets and others doing the voices. They can explore how many different versions of the story can be presented. The puppets need to follow the voices.

KS2 EXAMPLE   **Animal voices**

Time: 10 minutes introduction/10 minutes planning/10 minutes sharing

Talk about animal characteristics. If they had voices what might they be like? What might they be like if one animal (e.g. a tiger) was interviewing another (e.g. a mouse) for a job? In fours, two animals and two voices plan a short scene of a job interview in which voices match actions.

4: Dynamic duos

This approach is where the children are in role in pairs. It is a useful way of working because it can take place in the classroom for short periods of time. It can be used for many purposes, in particular the use of more formal language for a specific situation and to provide material for follow-up writing. It is usually very tightly structured, with the teacher giving clear briefings beforehand, clear signals to begin (e.g. a count-down from five), an agreement that no one comes out of role until it is time, and a clear signal to indicate when that should happen (e.g. the shake of a tambourine). In other words, it is not an open-ended meandering, but a focused and specific piece of work in which the teacher is observing and has specific expectations.

KS1 EXAMPLE   **Making a telephone enquiry**

Time: 3 minutes

After a whole-class discussion about wildlife parks, ask the children to consider how they would need to speak on the telephone to make an enquiry about the animals if they were making a special TV programme. What questions would they need to ask and how would they ask them? How should the person who works at the park answer such enquiries? Should they, as part of their job, speak in particular ways? Sitting back to back, Child A rings Child B to find out certain details from a local wildlife park. After two minutes, get them to change roles. Giving feedback on 'good practice' might precede a repeat of the conversation in which they try to improve their first attempt.

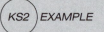 EXAMPLE **Reasoned argument**

Time: 5 minutes

After a whole-class introduction on the issues of new building development on green-field sites, the children take on the roles in pairs of (a) the politician who wants to provide more housing and (b) the headteacher of a country village school who is concerned about the diminishing sites in his/her area. The role-play is of a radio discussion in which each has to express their views and debate the issues. The importance of turn-taking, making points clearly and giving reasons for disagreeing with the views of others should all be discussed before going into role. This might be followed up with one pair volunteering to replay their efforts for the whole class, who would then be invited to comment on what was effective and why.

5: Freeze frame

When restructuring improvisations, the children could consider sometimes freezing the action for dramatic effect. Freeze frames can sometimes be accompanied by commentary or sound-bites.

 EXAMPLE **The emergency services**

Time: 15 minutes

Select four children to pretend they are someone who has been knocked off their bicycle, paramedics who have arrived to help and an onlooker in the street. Encourage them to play out the scene. Preparatory work may have been carried out in an earlier part of the topic, or while looking at non-fiction books as a class prior to this activity. Freeze the action every now and then and ask the other children questions such as: 'Look at this old lady's face. What do you think she is thinking?' 'What do you think the paramedics need to do next?' This is a vehicle to stimulate talk by creating action in the classroom, and stopping it at various points in order to focus the thinking.

(KS2) EXAMPLE   **In the news**

Time: 20 minutes

In preparation for writing newspaper reports, give out sample articles with photos from your local newspaper. In groups, replicate the photo as a freeze frame. Bring the freeze frame to life by counting down to 'action' so that the children are improvising what they think might have happened next (i.e. bringing the photo to life). Freeze frame the action again at certain points until the 'photo' is very different. How will the news report change? You will probably need to demonstrate this first with one group.

6: Guided action

Guided action is usually a whole-class activity, although another adult working with a small group might also use this outside the classroom. The teacher narrates a series of imagined events into which the children enter and participate. The teacher is not in role for this, but maintains control via the commentary. Guided action allows you to structure the activity tightly because you are describing actions and imaginings in great detail. However, it can also offer opportunities for more open-ended work stimulated by the preliminary instructions. For example, you may have talked the children through a walk across fields, over stiles, over stepping stones across a river. You will have described trees, hedgerows, animals, warm sun on their faces and the cool grass against their feet. Then you might ask them, in groups of four, to find a suitable spot for a picnic, and to start unpacking all the things they have brought with them. In this way, you have established the mode of working, provided lots of starting points to assist their imaginings, and set up a framework for them to develop their own ideas from there. Guided action can be used in many different ways, ranging from a short five-minute experience as an introduction to a discussion, to a longer exploration which eventually leads into a whole-class spontaneous improvisation with you in role.

(KS1) EXAMPLE   **Use of geographical terms (hill, river, stream, track, road etc.)**

Time: 5 minutes guided action/5 minutes teacher in role

You will need a large space such as the hall or playground. Explain to the children that they are going to follow the journey that Goldilocks took when she discovered the house of the three bears. Each child should find a space so that they can work independently. Talk them through walking down the path of Goldilocks's house, opening and closing the gate, off down the track, the birds singing, coming to the main road, crossing carefully to the other side, into the forest and so on. As you describe this journey, you will be able to use terminology that you have introduced as part of your geography work, for example over a hill, round a farm, through a wood, across a river or stream. Once they have reached the three bears' house, tell them that they now have to find their way back with a partner, this time without your help. Before they start out, discuss all the features of the journey to remind them, getting as many of the answers from them as possible. When they are safely back at the house they should sit in the garden and have an imaginary glass of juice and a piece of cake while they are waiting for everyone else to settle! Praise those who do this well. This activity could be used as a preliminary stimulus to map drawing as well as promoting speaking and listening.

(KS2) EXAMPLE   ## A voyage with Francis Drake

Time: 10 minutes preparation/10 minutes guided action

Show the children pictures of Elizabethan ships and discuss the conditions on board. Describe the sorts of provisions that needed to be stored on board, and the length of time they were at sea. In the hall, ask the children to lie on their backs and close their eyes. Describe their journey back through time (recorded music can help to set the atmosphere). Then describe the scene of a port. When they open their eyes they are there and need to get to work. Talk them through a range of activities one at a time, such as rolling barrels of water up the gang planks, driving sheep on board into pens, carrying sacks of flour and so on. All the time, your voice is acting as narrator to their movements. Make it as dramatic as you can! Move on to pulling in the gang planks, hauling up the anchor, untying ropes on the dock side and raising the sails. As the ship sails off into the dark night, those on watch take up their posts, but your children have to take their sleep. They make their way down the ladders into the depths of the ship and climb into their hammocks, tightly packed, side by side, and eventually silence falls. The music, or any other pre-agreed signal, brings them slowly back to the present. This could be used as a starting point for writing such as poetry about the feelings of those leaving home, or a captain's diary. Alternatively, you may allow the children to continue the imagining as a spontaneous improvisation in groups of four, in order to develop a story of something that happens on board.

7: Guided imagery

This is very similar to guided action, but the children remain seated or lie on the floor, with their eyes closed, and imagine what you describe. This technique is often used as a preliminary to discussion or improvisation. Your voice narrates, asking the children to imagine . . . Sometimes you might leave spaces for them to fill in pictures or ideas of their own. It is important to speak quite slowly and quietly when using this method so that the children are encouraged to concentrate.

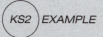

KS1 EXAMPLE — Journey down a rabbit hole

Time: 3 minutes guided imagery/5 minutes discussion

'Now that you have your eyes closed, try to picture a lovely green field. It has long grass, dandelions, tall trees around the edges, waving gently in the breeze . . . Suddenly, you see a little brown rabbit sitting up and looking round. He starts to run towards the trees. You are following him quietly, and you see him disappear into a hole between the roots of a huge tree. As you stare at the tree, you realise that the tree is getting bigger, and bigger, and bigger. No! It's you who are becoming smaller and smaller and smaller and smaller. The rabbit hole now looks like a huge cave, dark, a long tunnel stretching out before you. How do you feel? (PAUSE) Now you are starting to walk slowly into the tunnel . . .' etc.

KS2 EXAMPLE — The scrap yard

Time: 5 minutes guided imagery/10 minutes discussion

Take them on a journey to a scrap yard, but include lots of pauses for them to think up their own responses, e.g. 'As you stare at the piles and piles of old, rusty cars, what else do you see?' or 'Something starts to emerge from the rubbish slowly. What do you see?' This could be used as a stimulus to creating freeze frames making statements about the environment.

8: Hot seating

For this approach, the only person or people in role are those in 'the hot seat'. The hot seat is the place where a person sits to be questioned by pupils. It can take place as a whole-class activity or in smaller numbers with various hot-seated characters around the room being questioned by smaller groups of pupils. The person in the hot seat could be the teacher in role, a child in role, a group of children in role or a visitor in role. The role played might be a character from fiction, a historical character, a famous person or an imaginary person, depending on why this approach has been selected. It is an excellent way of getting children to ask questions to seek information, use information or explore inferred meaning. It provides an opportunity to frame questions, listen to the questions of others, hear replies and extend thinking beyond the known.

EXAMPLE   **Exploration beyond the text**

Time: 10 minutes

After reading a story to the whole class, explain that you are going to pretend to be the main character – it is a good idea to have a prop relating to the story to assist with this. Choose a child to take over as teacher. They will introduce you and invite children with their hands up to ask questions. Make it clear to the children when you are in and out of role, e.g. by changing seats or removing the prop. Once you return to being yourself, give feedback on the questions they asked and discuss the fact that so much more happens in stories than just the bits we read!

 EXAMPLE   **Victorian child labour**

Time: 10 minutes preparation/10 minutes hot seating

Provide the children with information (books/worksheets/pictures) on Victorian child labour. Explain that they have 10 minutes in which to become 'experts' and that four children will be selected to go into the hot seat for questioning by the rest of the class. They will be in role as Victorian children. At this stage, do not tell them who! After 10 minutes, gather the whole class together, having placed four chairs at the front. Select four children and put them by the door while you explain that these time travellers have kindly come along to answer questions. Explain that you will be listening to the questions carefully to see how much they have learned. After the hot seating, give feedback on how the questions were asked and answered, and ask the children to comment on what they have learned.

9: Improvisation: spontaneous

This approach can be used for small groups or the whole class. It can take place after a short instruction from the teacher or as a follow-on activity after guided action or imagery. The children go into role and make up the action spontaneously, allowing the story to develop in ways that are totally unplanned. It is important to establish three agreed ground rules when using this approach.

1. Have a clear signal to indicate when they are in role and not in role so that you can maintain control quickly and effectively (see Chapter 3 for more on classroom management techniques).

2. Explain that coming out of role is not an option during the improvisation because this spoils the illusion for others in the group. Reassure them that, if things start to go wrong, they can solve the problem as the characters, rather than reverting to self!

3. Encourage the children to build on each other's ideas rather than ignoring them. In other words, one person's 'discovery' can become a shared experience for the group.

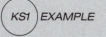 **EXAMPLE**   **Using language appropriate to a role or situation**

Time: 5 minutes introduction/10 minutes improvisations

In this example you might be discussing with the children how you should talk to a shop assistant when you are taking something back for a refund. First discuss the situation and then ask the children about how one should speak in this situation. Choose two children to improvise for the rest of the class. Repeat three times with different pairs of children, then let them all have a try back at their tables. Give a countdown so they know when to start pretending, and use a pre-arranged signal to call a halt. Give feedback.

KS2 EXAMPLE   **Exploring themes from a text**

Time: 10 minutes introduction/5 minutes improvisation/10 minutes discussion

Select a suitable chapter from your current class story that ends with a range of options open to the main character. Discuss the structure of chapter endings and the author's purpose in leaving it at a point of tension. Ask the children for their predictions about what might happen in the following chapter. Ask for volunteers to improvise a possible event from the next 'scene'. Show several options and discuss the implications of each in terms of the whole story development. Discuss the characters as portrayed in the improvisations. Were they behaving appropriately? How do authors maintain characters' responses? etc.

10: Improvisation: reconstructed

This approach is a development of the previous one. It enables the children to go back over their initial improvisation and shape it into a more polished practised piece either to show to others or to use as a basis for writing scripts or stories. The initial spontaneous improvisation serves the purpose of getting the ideas to flow, and this reconstruction process provides the opportunity to select and shape those ideas for an end-product. This involves moving into a more theatrical mode, in which the children are making informed decisions about how they create, structure and communicate work for performance to others.

Assembly on kindness to others (Personal, Social, Health and Emotional education [PSHE])

KS1 EXAMPLE

Time: 10 minutes reconstruction

After spontaneous improvisations of playground scenes, discuss with the children how bad behaviour incidents can be 'put right', and who the real superstars are in such situations. Reconstruct the bad incident and the person putting it right (e.g. saying sorry, sharing a snack, asking someone to join in the game). Replay the children's ideas, using their own words, but also asking them if they need to change any of it to show in assembly. Repeat to practise and put into a running order. It is also a good idea for the children to freeze into 'statues' after they have had their turn. The final format would be: run on, play the scene, freeze; next group run on, play their scene, freeze; etc. You might like to ask them what message they could all say together at the end. Young children can come up with some wonderful ideas of their own if they are given the space and freedom to do so!

Victorian family entertainment

KS2 EXAMPLE

Time: 20 minutes

In groups of four or five, the children should use information books to find out how the Victorians entertained themselves in the evenings without television. It would be important, of course, to discuss the distinctions between rich, middle-class and poor families. Allow them to choose roles to play and improvise scenes to demonstrate their findings. They should then evaluate these and reconstruct them into a smooth-running format, possibly with a narrator.

11: Masks

Masks offer a wonderful opportunity for children to explore and express emotions and actions through movement and gesture. They can be used with and without language. They also provide a 'safe haven' for children who are reluctant to speak but are keen to participate. Clearly, designing and making masks offers obvious links with other curriculum areas, particularly art, design technology and history. There is much scope for using masks within other drama techniques, for example when hot seating. See also Chapter 8 for further discussion on the use of masks with children who are learning English as an additional language.

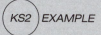 **EXAMPLE**

Characterisation in the role-play area

Time: ongoing

Providing masks in the role-play area can give encouragement to children to take on the roles of imagined characters. The masks help in two ways. First, they can remind the wearer of who they are and give confidence to the role. Second, they act as a stimulus to others who see the mask, because the wearer is presenting a stronger visual image. It is a good idea to provide a safety mirror so that children can see themselves.

KS2 EXAMPLE

Mood masks

Time: preparation 20 minutes; performance five minutes per group

This could have wider links to work on the Ancient Greeks or PSHE. Having made masks that portray specific emotions (sadness, joy, envy, guilt) explore movements that will extend the expression of these through action. Ask them to carry out certain actions in their mood (digging the garden, eating a banana, writing a letter) – this helps the children to really focus on how their movements affect the visual image of the character. It is therefore important to allow them to watch each other and evaluate each other's work constructively. Allow the children time to interview each other to see why they are sad, joyful, guilty etc. This could then lead to the writing of character descriptions.

12: Mime

Situations are presented through actions and facial expression but without speech. This might involve one pupil presenting something for the rest of the class to guess, it might be a pair of pupils planning a sequence of events, or it could be a larger group showing a situation or story. In other words, it is an 'end-product', just as a piece of writing or painting is the culmination of much useful preparatory planning, discussion, research and evaluation. These processes are the valuable part of the work. The mime itself can be a vehicle for the learning process, or the central focus of the learning as an art form. Mime is also useful for encouraging children to pay attention to finer detail in communication.

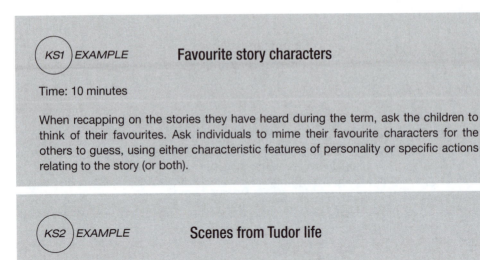

KS1 EXAMPLE — **Favourite story characters**

Time: 10 minutes

When recapping on the stories they have heard during the term, ask the children to think of their favourites. Ask individuals to mime their favourite characters for the others to guess, using either characteristic features of personality or specific actions relating to the story (or both).

KS2 EXAMPLE — **Scenes from Tudor life**

Time: 15 minutes

As a consolidation process of work completed on this history theme, ask the children, in groups of five or six, to prepare a mime of a typical Tudor scene, including as much detail as possible. The rest of the class should describe what they think is happening, and the performing group should explain where they found their information.

13: Performance

As discussed earlier in this chapter, the notion of 'performance' takes us into a different emphasis for the drama. Rather than improvisational techniques that are not necessarily repeated, a performance is perhaps repeated several times as further improvements and/or rehearsal takes place. Although at one level it could be argued that a performance is for the benefit of the audience, in primary schools the processes involved in creating the performance can be as important as the product itself. Initial exploratory drama techniques might be used in preparation for the performance, shaping ideas and storyline when there is no script as a starting point. Likewise, improvisations can assist the children in their understandings of characters with scripted drama. Such processes are important aspects of learning about communication in this art form.

Developing performance in schools is covered in more detail in Chapter 9, where theatre skills and practical knowledge are discussed. It is important to include performance as part of your planning for drama. It can be included in a discrete arts programme, as an extension of drama in English to develop communication skills, or simply to share the learning in other curricular areas. The performance element in itself can vary in scale, from the simple showing of ideas, through repeated improvisation, structured improvisation and script production, to fully rehearsed productions. Even these last can be on a small or a grand scale. It will all depend on what is appropriate to the intended learning outcomes at the time.

| KS1 EXAMPLE | **Performance in assembly of one of Aesop's Fables to illustrate an aspect of social behaviour** |

| KS2 EXAMPLE | **Alternative version of *Macbeth*, written and performed by Year 6 for parents and carers at the end of a topic on the Tudors** |

14: Puppets

The making and using of puppets offers much to the primary curriculum. Benefits include:

- the exploration of language through play
- asking and answering questions
- exploring or discussing emotions
- shaping story into performance
- exploration and extension of known stories
- creation of new stories
- associated technology activities (designing and making).

It is not just the children who can use puppets in their drama. Puppets can provide a useful mechanism for you to communicate with your class, or with smaller groups. Introducing a new idea, generating discussion, or opening up the children's curiosity are all examples of why a puppet might be used by you. A sad puppet will evoke different responses from an angry puppet, for example. Puppets are particularly good for children who feel less confident about expressing themselves because the puppet is like a mask behind which they can hide. There is a distancing effect which helps the work to feel 'safer' (which is why puppets are often used by psychologists with children to help them talk about difficult issues). There are different ways of making puppets. For example:

- lollystick puppets – a card head with hair pasted to a flat lollipop stick
- paper bag puppets – draw a face on a white paper bag and use as a glove
- finger puppets – make a face or whole body in card and paste a card loop to the back so you can insert a finger; several can be used by one person at the same time
- balloon heads – covering a balloon with papier mâché then fastening a stick below and covering with cloth

- Plasticine modelling – design a head in Plasticine, cover with papier mâché, attach cloth and use as a glove with fingers inside the head

- cloth puppets – attach cloth to a polystyrene ball

- shadow puppets – card silhouettes on thin sticks to play against a light, creating shadows on the wall

- commercial puppets – these are available everywhere from wildlife parks to toy shops, including string puppets, glove puppets and finger puppets

- reading scheme puppets – many publishers sell characters to accompany stories in their schemes.

Working towards a performance can be fun with puppets, but don't forget that they can also be used for everyday language play, phonics work and improvisation.

 KS1 *EXAMPLE*   **The puppet with a problem!**

Time: 10 minutes

Introduce the children to your sad puppet. Invite the children to ask the puppet questions about why he feels sad. It emerges that he is very worried because his owner has recently had a new gas fire installed and this means that Father Christmas will not be able to get down the chimney. Use the puppet to help the children solve this problem in pairs.

KS2 *EXAMPLE*   **Life in Roman times**

Time: 30 minutes research/20 minutes making puppets/30 minutes devising the presentation

Use research skills to find facts about the Romans using non-fiction books and the Internet. In groups, make speedy lollystick puppets to enact different aspects of life in Roman times.

15: Radio plays

The potential here is enormous: documentaries, plays, dramatised stories, interviews and so on. A practical advantage of working in sound only is that it can take place round a table in the classroom, and the eventual goal of recording then playing back the product is an excellent way to focus children's minds! It is important to let children hear examples of the particular type of programme before expecting them to create something in the same genre. Creating sound effects and music is another enjoyable aspect of this approach.

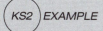 *EXAMPLE* **Making a story recording**

Time: 30 minutes

Many KS1 classrooms have talking books or dramatised stories to which children can listen through headphones. Having enjoyed these, children will relish the prospect of making their own by recording onto a computer. This gives them a real reason to practise reading with fluency and expression, and listening to the recordings provides opportunities for self-evaluation. Playing a child's recording to the rest of the class can also be a real incentive and reward for good work.

EXAMPLE **News broadcast**

Having discussed and established particular stylistic aspects of news broadcasts, get the children to write their own news about things, real or invented, that have been happening in school.

16: Reader in role

Reading in role can be used to help children develop concepts of the many functions of reading. It can also provide a particularly helpful framework for reluctant readers who perhaps lack confidence in more formal reading situations. Use of this technique can range from children pretending to read a newspaper in the home corner to a 'news-reader' reading a script for the camera. The wider potential of reading in role is discussed in Chapter 7 along with further examples.

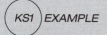 *EXAMPLE* **Reading the register**

Time: 5 minutes

Young children usually love pretending to be a teacher! Provide a laminated list of names with a sheet for ticking attached. As the child calls out the names and ticks, you can mark the official version! A different child can call and mark the laminated register each day.

KS2 EXAMPLE **Science documentary**

Time: 40 minutes preparation/10 minutes showing time

Organise the children to work in groups of four or five for this task, preferably each group on a different day of the week in order to space out the showing times. Together they will research a particular aspect of a science topic that is part of the current classroom work (e.g. Electricity Now and Then). This should include reports on experiments, background knowledge from textbooks and the Internet, and mock interviews as appropriate. They prepare a TV documentary to perform to the rest of the class. For this they will need to write a clear script which they will read and perform.

17: Role-play area

The role-play area is a familiar sight in many Reception and KS1 classrooms. As the traditional home corner, dressing-up clothes, home implements and child-sized furniture provide a setting for young children to play out family roles. This imaginative play can help to develop their oracy and social skills. Reading and writing opportunities can contribute to learning in a well-planned home corner: telephone directories, computers, message pads, cookery books, calendars and food packets all have a part to play. Role-play areas can also be transformed into a variety of themed areas, usually to link with a particular aspect of work in the curriculum: shops, cafe, fire station, post office, dentist's surgery, space station, igloo and so on. The quality of the learning which takes place through such play depends very much on the quality of the provision. For example, placing special 'props' that relate to a story you have just read to the class will encourage the children to play the characters from the story, extend and adapt the storyline and so on. Adult modelling of language and imaginative play when participating with children in role-play areas are also a vital aspect of the provision. At KS2, role-play areas tend to be more structured according to the intended learning, but there is no doubt that even Year 6 children enjoy the opportunity to create their own stories and dramas, especially when allowed to dress up!

KS1 EXAMPLE **Garden centre and shop as part of a topic on plants**

18: Script work

Reading parts and acting from scripts is one way of organising group reading. It can promote fluency and expression by justifying the rereading process and giving a meaningful context to the reading. Where scripts have stage directions, this offers an additional opportunity to read for meaning, in which the children are required to 'practise' the script and follow the stage directions as they do so. Popular reading schemes provide play script texts as part of their series. It is also great fun to use scripts that have been written by the children themselves and this is an ideal way of linking reading, writing and speaking together. More is included on this in Chapters 5, 6 and 7.

19: Writer in role

Putting the children into role to write can not only provide more purposeful contexts for the writing; it can also be tremendously motivating by adding an element of context and fun. The writing activity might be for individuals or larger groups; for example writing telephone messages in the role-play area or composing a group letter-in-a-bottle from a whole class who are marooned on a tropical island! This technique will be discussed more extensively in Chapter 6, but the examples here illustrate how using drama can really help to bring the writing alive and thus motivate even the most reluctant of writers.

KS1 *EXAMPLE*   **Planning a teddy bears' picnic**

Time: 10 minutes whole-class discussion/10 minutes writing

Now that Goldilocks has made friends with the three bears, they have decided to plan a grand picnic party for all the teddies in the area. In groups of four, each child taking one of the four roles, ask the children to make a list. These could be differentiated according to ability groups; for instance one group might be making a list of foods, whereas another group might be writing the timetable or invitations for the picnic.

EXAMPLE **TV script writing**

Time: 20 minutes preparation/20 minutes writing/20 minutes feedback

Explain that many soap operas are written by teams of script writers. Show the last 10 minutes of a favourite series such as *Neighbours* or *Hollyoaks*. Hold a whole-class discussion, with you in role as the series editor, to brainstorm ideas about the next episode, including such issues as plot development and character motivation. Divide the children into script-writing teams of three and allow 20 minutes for writing. Pair up each team with another team, and in turn ask each team to read the script aloud. The other team then gives feedback on the script in role as the editing directors.

20: Simulation

A simulation involves improvisation but is less spontaneous because it involves elements of planning and preparation that lead to known outcomes. The children might or might not be involved in that planning and preparation. Simulation is a useful process to use when the teacher also wishes to be in role. Before starting, the teacher explains to the children exactly what is going to happen. This may involve the children in setting up the room in a particular way. Other preparations may include research from information books, character planning, the gathering of costumes or props and so on. The children will know what is going to happen before the commencement of the simulation. The value of this approach is that it provides opportunities for certain types of experiences in which children can speak, listen and observe within a situation to which they might not normally have access.

KS1 *EXAMPLE* **A Christian wedding**

Time: 10 minutes preparation/10 minutes simulation

Discuss love, marriage and weddings from different religions, and ask for information from the children about the weddings they have attended. What similarities are there between weddings from different religions? Describe the main features of a Christian wedding, look at pictures together, then ask the children how the room could be set to create a church. Arrange the chairs accordingly, with a table for the altar, flowers, Bible etc. Decide who is going to be who: bride, groom, parents, bridesmaids, relations, vicar, choir etc. It is probably a good idea for you to take the role of vicar so that you are in a position to maintain control. Insist that once they are in the church area they must keep pretending to be the person they have chosen. Allow them to arrive gradually. A CD of organ music could help to set the atmosphere if you can obtain one. Edit the service appropriately so that it doesn't last too long. Singing one verse of each hymn will help here! After the event, discuss issues arising, such as the significance of festivals, religion and love, promises, emotions, listening supportively etc. Use terminology throughout this session which does not assume stereotypes; for example 'Some people choose to get married', 'Some couples who get married decide to get married in a church' rather than 'When you all get married' etc.

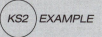 **EXAMPLE**

Protest meeting about a proposed multi-storey car park

Time: 10 minutes preparation/20 minutes simulation

In the context of study on the influence of local developments on human activities, tell the children that a multi-storey car park is to be built in the centre of a small country town. Show them a map on a large flip chart or overhead projection with key features of the town, roads and the site of the new car park. To make it really controversial you could even decide that it will be built on the site of a playing field!

Divide the children into groups of three, and give them a card with information such as: 'You are from the town council. You want this to go ahead because it will bring more trade to the town.' 'You are parents of local schoolchildren. You are worried that the planned site will mean more traffic along the road where your children walk to school.' Allow the children five minutes to plan their arguments, and also to build up character profiles about themselves: age, job, personality, views etc. Discuss with the children how the room would be arranged for a public meeting in the Town Hall, and move chairs and tables accordingly. Ensure that there is an effective chairperson, and brief the children on the procedures of addressing all comments to the chair. You should choose to take a role yourself from which you can steer the debate from within. Allow them to enter the meeting room area gradually. Someone could be serving imaginary tea and coffee as they arrive. Such a debate could be a preliminary to listing the pros and cons of such developments, or writing letters of support or complaint.

21: Tableaux

This is an immensely useful technique, because it makes very tightly structured demands of the children within a limited time-frame, and yet it offers them much scope for the development of their own ideas. A tableau is a still and silent scene or abstract representation of a theme created by a group of people. In a drama context, this group might be the whole class, with the children joining the tableau one at a time as you build up an idea, event or picture collaboratively. Alternatively, they might be working in groups of five or six to make a tableau, or sequence of tableaux. As this work takes place, they will be discussing ideas, possibly using books to discover information, planning, sequencing, evaluating, modifying and so on. The tableaux approach can also be useful as a follow-on to guided imagery, when you have been asking the children to focus on a specific theme which they go on to discuss in groups, then present in this form. Much learning is taking place during the development process, and the finished product is the evidence of their work as an art form.

KS1 EXAMPLE   **Exploration of purposes for reading**

Time: 5 minutes discussion/10 minutes tableaux examples

Discuss with the children how important reading is, and all the different reasons why children and adults read. In groups of three, ask them to make a tableau of a reading situation (e.g. library, newspaper on the bus, letter, teacher reading child's work) for the rest of the class to guess. Give them just one minute to 'plan in secret' without the other groups hearing them. Remind them that, because they won't be allowed to speak or move, they will need to give lots of clues with their positions and their faces. Watch, guess and discuss!

KS2 EXAMPLE   **Greek mythology**

Time: 30 minutes preparation/3 minutes per group showing time

Using their prior knowledge of Greek mythology, ask each group to select a particular story. They should read and research the story first, then plan three tableaux to present the key scenes or events: start, middle and end. As an extension activity, each tableau could be linked by planned movement, music or speech if there is additional time for this.

22: Teacher in role

Several of the approaches that have been described so far have mentioned teacher in role. This can be a useful way to work because it can:

- help to direct the drama
- provide useful information for the children
- enable you to model certain types of language
- give credibility to the use of imagination and pretence.

Important guidance on how to maintain control of the class while in role is offered in Chapter 3, including clear boundaries between you and the role, use of props and positioning, directing from within, observing from within and so on.

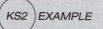 **KS1** EXAMPLE   **Writing to the sad toys**

Time: 10 minutes role-play/20 minutes writing

Pretending that you are a postman/woman you explain that you are very concerned about the toys in the toy shop who have been upset because they never get any letters. In role you ask for volunteers to write to different toys (some of whom you might have brought along to introduce to the children).

KS2 EXAMPLE   *The Secret Garden*

Time: 10 minutes video/20 minutes role-play

The children have been watching an excerpt from *The Secret Garden* (Warner Home Video UK Limited, 1994) and comparing it with a chapter in the book first published in 1911 (Hodgson Burnett, 2007). You explain that the author, who died in 1924, is going to travel forward in your class time machine to hear about their opinions of how the director has interpreted her book and made it into a film. How will she respond to all the changes in the world, especially the concept of film and sound? You take on the role of the author and conduct your lesson from her perspective. This will be slightly different from hot seating because you will be asking the children questions and asking them to carry out tasks as the author.

23: Television and film

Involving children in activities linked to popular culture is an obvious way of motivating and engaging their interest. There is also an extraordinary amount of scope for learning through these media. Television and film can be used as a stimulus, a model, a focus for analysis or an end-product for children's own work using video camera. Editing software provides further scope for discussion, planning and the creation and expression of ideas into a structure to be communicated to others. It is far too extensive an area to describe in detail here, but neither is it rocket science! Consider it as an option.

 KS1 EXAMPLE   **A tour of our school**

Time: small group sessions of 30 minutes to piece together

Plan and film a commentary on different parts of the school for new children or to email to children in another town or country if you have community links.

KS2 EXAMPLE   **Topic documentary**

Time: ongoing

Use the filming of a 'documentary' about the current topic in history, science or geography as a target for the production of research, writing and presentation. This could be linked across to other areas of the curriculum: for example, making props, illustrations or editing clips from the Internet. Different groups could contribute to the whole, or a short film (to make a whole series) could be produced by each group.

The different techniques described in this chapter have different advantages in terms of reading, writing, speaking and listening. Each of the techniques is listed in Table 2.1 to show which are particularly useful for different aspects of learning English skills.

TABLE 2.1 Application of the 23 techniques for learning different English skills

TECHNIQUE	PRACTISING SPEECH	DISCUSSION	LISTENING SKILLS	READING AS PREPARATION	READING SCRIPTS	FOLLOWING INSTRUCTIONS	WRITING FOR PLANNING	WRITING AFTER THE STIMULUS	WRITING IN ROLE	WRITING EVALUATIONS
1: Conscience alley	✓	✓	✓	✓				✓		
2: Dance-drama	✓	✓		✓						✓
3: Detached voices	✓	✓	✓	✓	✓		✓		✓	
4: Dynamic duos	✓	✓	✓		✓			✓	✓	
5: Freeze frame	✓	✓		✓				✓		✓
6: Guided action			✓			✓		✓		
7: Guided imagery			✓			✓		✓		
8: Hot seating	✓	✓	✓	✓				✓		✓
9: Improvisation: spontaneous	✓	✓						✓		
10: Improvisation: reconstructed	✓	✓						✓	✓	
11: Masks	✓	✓	✓	✓	✓					✓
12: Mime	✓	✓		✓						✓
13: Performance	✓	✓		✓	✓	✓	✓			✓
14: Puppets	✓	✓	✓	✓	✓	✓	✓			✓
15: Radio plays	✓	✓	✓		✓		✓			✓
16: Reader in role	✓	✓		✓		✓		✓		
17: Role-play area	✓	✓		✓	✓	✓	✓		✓	
18: Script work	✓	✓								
19: Writer in role				✓		✓		✓	✓	
20: Simulation		✓	✓					✓		✓
21: Tableaux		✓								✓
22: Teacher in role			✓			✓		✓		
23: Television and film	✓	✓	✓	✓	✓	✓	✓		✓	✓

Management and organisation

Chapter overview

This chapter aims to provide a practical approach to planning how to use drama techniques in your classroom and elsewhere. It discusses:

- structure and organisation
- classroom management techniques
- different ways of grouping
- using different spaces
- the importance of timing
- useful resources for drama.

Structure and organisation

Planning how to organise and manage drama activities requires you to consider three main components: first, the *content* that will be based upon curriculum requirements and your knowledge of the children's learning needs; second, the *approach* (mode of drama) that will most suit the required learning; and, finally, the *organisation and management* of the session – how you will actually get the session to work effectively, whether it is a five-minute drama stimulus or an afternoon developing ideas to present in assembly. It is this third component, classroom management, that we shall examine in this chapter.

The interactive and sometimes open-ended nature of drama does not mean that it has to be disorganised or out of control. It is true that badly planned drama activities can lead to chaos, with very little relevant learning taking place, even if the children have a wonderful time! Just like other subjects, drama needs a clear focus on learning outcomes, and should operate through well-organised classroom management. Even if the lesson is open-ended to allow children's own ideas to flow, it is still important to plan carefully how this will be managed. The classroom management of drama should be designed according to the learning style or drama method taking place. For example, it might require a tight instructional approach whereby the teacher is leading a simulation with clear rules and boundaries. On the other hand, child-led improvisations are more free-flowing but nevertheless require focused preparation, specific time limits, clear goals set, and reporting-back procedures to high expectations.

Classroom management techniques

Teacher roles and responsibilities

You will have many roles to play when leading drama activities, including taking on a character role yourself! You should also be:

- providing the necessary information, examples and resources to help the children's understanding
- showing them that you are prepared to take part in the make-believe
- explaining in ways that can be understood by all
- making clear your expectations and setting challenging but achievable targets
- giving feedback that extends the learning
- listening to the children's ideas and points of view
- ensuring that everyone has an equal opportunity to participate and learn to their maximum potential
- allowing time for children to reflect and evaluate.

When you adopt a role in character, your relationship with the children will change. It is therefore important to use management techniques that help you to maintain control despite the altered dynamic. It is helpful to remember the following rules to guide you:

1. Make firm divisions between you as teacher and you as character.
   Agree a clear signal to indicate when you are in role and when you are not (e.g. 'When I am sitting on that chair, I am the angry police inspector, but when I am on this chair I am back to being me').

2. Enter into the spirit of the pretence.
   Try to use voice and posture to create your role, but don't worry if you feel you can't act. The children will absolutely love the fact that you are joining in the make-believe, and will not be making judgements about your performance.

3. Use what you can to help you.
   Additional props or pieces of costume such as a hat or a shawl can help to create the illusion, and will also give you more confidence if you do feel a bit nervous. These can become part of the de-roling signal if you wish (i.e. 'When I take the hat off I am back to being me!').

TABLE 3.1 Functions of teacher in role

FUNCTION OF THE ROLE	EXAMPLES OF TEACHER'S ROLE
To set a problem or challenge	In role as a toy shop owner who keeps finding the toys in all the wrong places each morning
To provide information	In role as an escapee from a volcanic eruption where there are still people to be rescued
To act as a go-between	In role as a teddy bear who can talk to the organisers of a picnic on behalf of the other bears
To lead	In role as the lead investigator of a robbery
To intervene	In role as a 'boss' when the arguments between factory workers become too circuitous
To rescue	In role as a new character bringing additional information when the drama becomes 'stuck'
To model	In role as a politician in the House of Commons
To bring things to an end	In role as a caretaker, saying it is time for the meeting to finish, and asking them to decide if and when they need to meet again

4.   Remember that you can also maintain class control whilst in role.

A character can change the direction of the drama, so, if the crowd of Hamelin residents are wandering around aimlessly, you, in role as an irate baker, can leap onto your soap box and move the action forward by declaring, 'I am absolutely fed up of all this filth and disease. My flour sacks were eaten again last night! What we need round here are some decisions. Who is going to come with me to see the mayor about these rats?'

Working in role can operate at different levels. For instance, you might be in a controlling role (e.g. the Pied Piper) steering the drama from within, or you might be an observer (e.g. one of the following children). The level of input will vary according to the type of activity, the experience of the children and the themes on which you are working. It is certainly helpful to clarify the function of your input in your own mind when planning the session, but also remember that you might need to change or add to this during the drama if the need arises. Table 3.1 shows examples of the main functions of teacher in role.

Basic management strategies

The management techniques and tips outlined here are intended not as a definitive magical list, but rather as a useful starting point. They are based on the common sense of classroom management: high expectations, clear instructions, transparent rules, routines and structures; but in ways that do not lose the fun and enjoyment of learning!

Developing working rules collaboratively

Establishing clear working rules helps the drama to succeed because the children are clear about what is expected of them. It is better to have just a small number of rules that can be remembered. Wherever possible these should be developed with the children themselves. In this way they will have ownership of the rules and will also be more likely to remember them. Questions such as 'When you are working in groups how will you let the others know you want to say something?' or 'If you disagree with someone's idea, how is the best way to tell them?' actually encourage children to consider the reasons for the rules as well as the actual rules themselves.

Stopping and starting the action

When 30 children are all enthusiastically discussing and planning, inevitably there is noise! Shouting over such noise can often result in raising the volume rather than reducing it. There are certain techniques that you can build in to your lessons that will help you to regain the children's attention when required. One effective way to do this is to use a magic cushion (Years 1 to 3) or a control chair (Years 4 to 6). A suitably sparkly or patterned cushion should be placed in a prominent spot in the room where you are working. Explain to the children that when you sit on the cushion its magic draws them to you, and this is very handy if you need to gather them together for a new instruction! Praise them for arriving quickly and sitting quietly. Add to the fun and the pretence by showing how impressed you are that the 'magic' works! A 'control chair' follows the same rules but is more appropriate for older children. Explain to them that sometimes you will need to stop the busy group work and gather them together for further instructions or discussion. The challenge of spotting you on the special chair and responding to that signal as quickly as possible can add to the fun if you set a challenge to get there quickly and sensibly!

Group gathering

If the children are all busy working in groups, it is sometimes better to gather each group separately rather than calling the whole class at once. This can be done by visiting the groups first which seem to be near completion. Ask them about their work then instruct them to join you by the cushion or control chair. As these groups gradually move to the space and sit down, the others will usually realise that work has stopped and will join the rest.

Sound signals

A triangle chime, shake of the tambourine, beat of the drum, chord on the piano or something similar can be a signal to stop working and listen without moving away from their work space. An agreed sound such as this is far better than shouting over the tops of busy talking voices. Older children should be able to respond to different signals, for example a chime meaning stand still/stop talking, a tambourine meaning sit on the floor/stop talking, three drum beats meaning freeze, a chord on the piano meaning gather round on the carpet.

Countdown

Counting down from five or ten can be another way to focus children's attention, although beware of having to shout over the top of the noise – this usually only succeeds in raising the noise level! Counting down might be a signal to a point at which they freeze ('. . . three, two, one, freeze!'), or it can also be a signal for action to begin ('. . . three, two, one, ACTION!'). Changing the volume of your voice so it becomes louder as a build-up to action, or quieter as it focuses down to stillness, adds further control. As your voice becomes quieter, the children have to listen even harder.

Movement and stillness

Stillness can be as effective as movement. It is also a part of managing the drama. The following techniques can be useful for various drama methods, and children should be taught to respond to these in the very early stages so that they become established ways of working.

- *Freeze:* To freeze is to become still instantly and hold the position like a statue. It is important to teach children how to freeze properly by explaining that *everything* is still, including eyes and lips. It is also advisable to teach them not to focus their gaze on another person, as this can distract them and disturb the stillness. Encourage them to focus on an object, the wall or the floor.

- *Slow motion:* Moving in slow motion (like action replays on televised football) can bring dramatic focus to a performance, and can also be an exciting way to steer the action. Modelling this for the children can help them to understand that even blinking and turning the head have to be at a reduced speed. (Don't be afraid to demonstrate this. They love it when teacher joins in!) Slow motion can be a good way of linking sections of a drama, for example a journey back through time. It can also be useful for moving into and out of role, for example from a freeze position at the end of a piece to sitting on the carpet ready for discussion.

- *Choreographed movement:* When children need to link pieces together, for example a set of three tableaux, they should have the opportunity to plan their movements carefully. One way of approaching this is to ask them to plan the changeover in four separate movements, providing four drum beats to assist the process. Encourage them to work as a team, making links between their movements so that they create interesting shapes and directions.

Making time for all

If all children are to feel their work is valued and are to have the opportunity to perform and receive feedback it is important that no one be excluded. However, often time can run out and you are left with the problem of how to give the activity a satisfactory conclusion. There are certain management techniques that can be used to help solve this problem.

Sharing and showing work

If 30 children are sitting on the carpet all eagerly wanting to show their mime or share an idea, it can be frustrating and unproductive for them to sit for too long listening to just three or four chosen peers. Children need to be as active as possible for as much of the time as possible. Sometimes, time can be maximised by letting them show or tell to a partner (simultaneously). In this way, every child has an opportunity to engage and receive some feedback. Other ways of maximising the sharing and showing of work include the following.

- *Group to group*: If you have six groups, divide them into three lots of two and let them perform simultaneously to their partner group. You should circulate round all three and ensure that you can say something about each at the end.

- *Rotating the days*: When children are working in smaller groups towards a performance of their work, it can be appropriate to allow them to do this on different days. This helps solve the problem of space and also means that the presentation of their work can be spaced out during the course of the week.

- *Teacher envoys*: Select an individual child to watch each group as if they are the teacher, making it clear to everyone that at the end these envoys will each take a turn to report back to the whole class on what they have seen.

Calming down time

Children may need to calm down at the beginning of a session, for example if they have just come in from playtime, and they will always need to calm down and de-role at the end of the session. Not only is it disturbing for other classes to be interrupted by 30 Viking warriors rampaging back to their classroom, it is also going to affect the next learning activity if children's minds and bodies are still full of the drama. In some cases, for example if you have been dealing with more disturbing issues, it is also vital that the children have the opportunity to 'let go' of that and feel safe in the knowledge that they are now back in the normal school situation.

There are several techniques which you can use as calming and de-roling exercises. If there is enough space, let the children lie down and close their eyes. If not, let them sit comfortably with their eyes closed, out of reach of any other person.

- *Breathing and relaxation*: Ask them to focus their minds on the in-breath and the out-breath, counting silently to four on each out-breath, and then starting again. If any thoughts distract them, ask them to let go of each thought as if it is a balloon floating away and start the counting again from one.

- *Body relaxation*: Ask them to focus their thoughts on their feet. Make their feet feel heavy, relaxed, sinking into the floor. Next the ankles, and so on, right through the body until the whole body is relaxed.

- *Guided meditation*: Once the children are comfortable and quiet, talk them through an imagined scene; for example 'Try to picture a beautiful beach. You are lying on the beach. You can hear the waves gently lapping on the shore . . .'. Take them through a calming journey which eventually leads their minds back to the classroom.

- *De-roling:* While the children sit with their eyes closed, summarise where they have just finished, then talk them back into school. Explain what they are going to do next, for example 'When you get back to the classroom I would like you to get out your pencil and your maths book and finish the work on money that we started this morning.' Ask them to open their eyes, and in a very quiet voice ask them how they should return to the classroom and what they will do when they get there. Tell them that you are going to watch them closely to see how well they do this.

Different ways of grouping

Chapter 2 described the range of approaches to drama, each of which can require different types of groupings. The size and composition of a group significantly influences the success of the work, and careful thought needs to go into how these are created and why. Children can be grouped in different ways according to various criteria:

- ability
- age
- gender
- social skills
- friendship
- language
- specialisms.

When defining your groups, you need to consider why you are imposing the parameters. For example:

- *same ability* e.g. to differentiate according to learning needs
- *mixed ability* e.g. to learn from others or learn from explaining to others
- *similar age* e.g. to cater for age-related interest levels
- *different ages* e.g. to build in specific responsibilities
- *single gender* e.g. to cater for specific gender-related topics
- *mixed gender* e.g. more usual way of working
- *confident/less confident* e.g. to enable less confident children to work without being dominated
- *mixed* e.g. to help focus on different roles within a group (leader, conciliator, critic etc.)
- *children choosing* e.g. to develop an area of common interest
- *teacher choosing* e.g. to 'break up' unproductive collaborations

- *confident bilingual* e.g. where translations will broaden understanding and teach about language

- *first language* e.g. where children need to explore ideas in their first language before developing them in English

- *research* e.g. to work on an area of agreed common interest

- *expert* e.g. where certain specialisms are needed within a group

- *generic* e.g. where several different specialisms are needed in each group (editor, illustrator, reporter etc.).

When applying such criteria to your decisions about groupings, you need to be sure that your planning will assist the learning process. You should also be careful not to reinforce implicit stereotypes into your groupings, particularly in single gender groups (although *reversing* stereotypical roles can be a useful way to teach positively about issues of equal opportunities).

Group size

The size of a group has a considerable impact upon the learning that takes place. In other areas of the curriculum, productivity is far higher where children are grouped at tables of four rather than six or eight. In drama, the interaction sometimes requires more than four. The group size also impacts upon the number of groups you will have to manage and support. It is far easier to work your way round four groups of eight than eight groups of four, and this has major implications for your levels of input and feedback. However, at the same time you need to ensure that productivity is not impaired by groups that are too large.

It is quite feasible for some drama activities to take place in smaller groups when the rest of the class are doing other things. Art and drama go well together, and this has the added advantage of less clearing up if only half the class are using glue and paint! In this case you need to relate your selection of group size to the level of teacher involvement required. For instance, two groups of six children developing a scripted improvisation from previous work carried out with you in the hall might only require occasional input and checking from you, working for the most part independently. On the other hand, exploratory work with the whole class, and you in role, clearly requires you to be there 100 per cent of the time!

The following guidance is intended to help you consider the advantages of different group sizes.

- *Pairs:* excellent for interviews, telephone conversations, question and answer sessions etc. Pair work is very suitable when working in a small area, or at tables in the classroom.

- *Trios:* adds the opportunity to have an observer to give feedback at the end, or a referee in a debate.

- *Fours:* useful when the children are working independently from you. Also good to bring two pairs into a group of four after working together on initial planning, or to swap partners for reporting-back purposes.

- *Five/six:* advisable to use these larger group sizes only when the children are able to work competently in drama, possibly reserving this approach until KS2. Larger groups such as this are necessary where more characters are needed to create an improvisation or simulation.

- *Eight/ten:* can work well for more structured activities (e.g. practising a scripted play). It is advisable to have a designated leader for each group. High levels of teacher involvement are usually needed for larger groups.

- *Whole class:* requires total teacher involvement, either through guided imagery or by having teacher in role during improvisation, simulation etc.

Changing group size during the drama

It is sometimes appropriate and effective to reorganise the group sizes within the same drama activity so that the dynamics change to suit a particular stage of the process. Two examples of how this might happen are shown below.

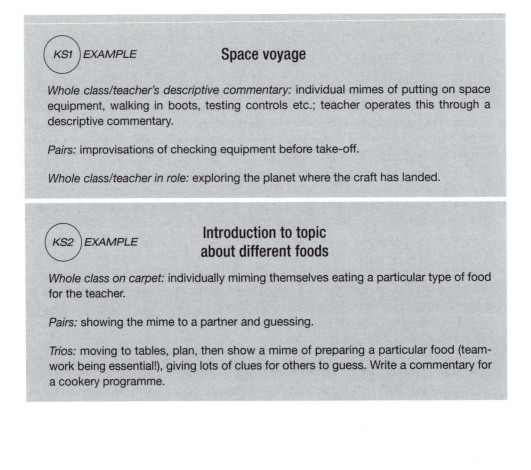

(KS1) EXAMPLE   **Space voyage**

Whole class/teacher's descriptive commentary: individual mimes of putting on space equipment, walking in boots, testing controls etc.; teacher operates this through a descriptive commentary.

Pairs: improvisations of checking equipment before take-off.

Whole class/teacher in role: exploring the planet where the craft has landed.

(KS2) EXAMPLE   **Introduction to topic about different foods**

Whole class on carpet: individually miming themselves eating a particular type of food for the teacher.

Pairs: showing the mime to a partner and guessing.

Trios: moving to tables, plan, then show a mime of preparing a particular food (teamwork being essential!), giving lots of clues for others to guess. Write a commentary for a cookery programme.

Group splitting

Purposeful splitting of groups can be of great assistance to activities where you require children to report or explain. Here are some examples of this technique.

- *Partner swaps:* where the children work in pairs, then split up and find a new partner to report or ask questions.

- *Incremental groups:* where smaller groups (e.g. pairs) are put together to form larger groups (e.g. into fours or sixes) in order to pool or compare ideas from their initial planning.

- *Rainbowing:* where the children work in one group, after which each child in the group is given a different colour. They then regroup into colour groups (with members of other groups), to report back, share, ask questions, seek information etc. This can be used as a device for moving from expert groups to generic groups and vice versa.

- *Envoying:* where a member of each group moves to a central group to report or seek information (e.g. different groups representing members of a community each send a representative to a central committee to make a decision).

Using different spaces

In large schools, where hall use is limited to a twice-weekly slot, it is understandable that dance, physical education and music will take priority. However, this is no reason for not including drama in your weekly plans – hall space is not essential to drama. A good working space can nearly always be created in the classroom (the playground can also be useful sometimes). Here are some ideas about how you might use your own classroom for drama by rearranging the furniture.

- *Open space:* clear tables and chairs, either using a special team at playtime (before the lesson) and lunchtime (after the lesson) or by 'training' the class to meet the challenge, timing them each week to see if they can improve their record speed! Be sure to discuss appropriate movement and lifting rules so that everyone works safely.

- *Carpet area:* if you have a carpeted reading corner in your classroom, this can be useful for introductory sessions, or showing work in progress or finished work. However, do bear in mind that when children have to sit in a cramped space for long periods they can become restless through no fault of their own – they are simply uncomfortable. If you know they will be sitting for longer than 10 minutes, it is usually worth making a circle of chairs instead.

- *Role-play area:* as well as using this area for actual role-play, it can also be a handy space to use when children are preparing something in an independent group to show later to the rest of the class.

- *Alternative arrangements of tables and chairs:* the existing furniture in your classroom can be used to create all sorts of scenarios. Some examples are shown in Figure 3.1. The moving of chairs and tables can help to solve the space problem, but also

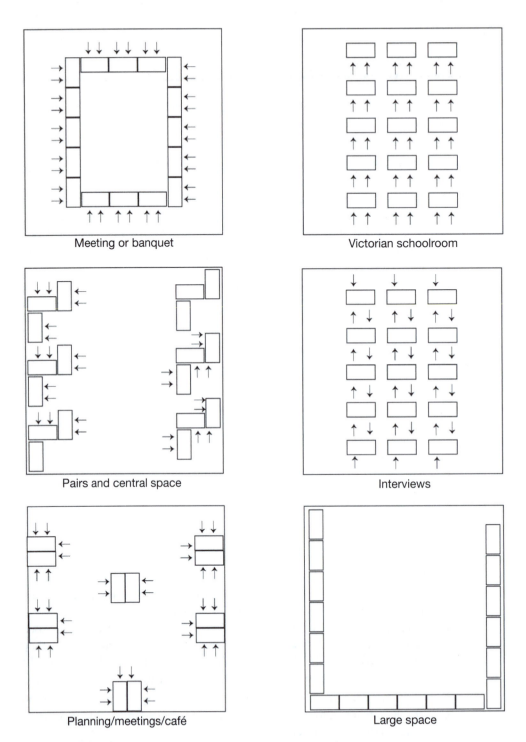

FIGURE 3.1 Alternative scenarios available by rearranging your classroom.

serves to create the illusion of a different scene. This is usually very appealing to children and can add to the excitement and realism of the drama.

The importance of timing

Drama doesn't necessarily need a long and sustained period of time. Input for supporting your teaching of English can vary in the time taken from five to 35 minutes. A five-minute mime can be a good introduction to generating ideas for writing lists. Researching to create a tableau might be a 10-minute task as part of the use of non-fiction texts. Working with scripts provides a multitude of opportunities for reading and writing. In other words, the drama might take place at the start, during or at the end of another lesson as a means of supporting learning.

If you are planning a drama session that is likely to last for longer than half an hour, it is important to plan how much time you will allow for each of the different sections (e.g. five minutes warm-up, five minutes individual improvisation, ten minutes pair work, ten minutes reporting back). It is also essential that you make time limits clear to the children and stick to these so that your high expectations are consistent. Prompts such as 'You have only five minutes to create your tableaux' and 'You have two minutes left' all help to keep them on task.

A certain amount of astute fine-tuning is also a key skill of good teaching. If children are left for too long on a particular activity they will usually become bored, which inevitably leads to off-task behaviour. Don't be afraid to set additional challenges, go into role to change the way things are moving, or call the class back together for a reminder or review if you feel this is necessary. The unpredictability of some drama sessions requires that you may have to make changes to your original plans to enable the progress of the drama to lead to useful learning outcomes. Ongoing informal assessment and related fine-tuning such as this can play an important part in supporting the learning.

Useful resources for drama

It is a good idea to build up a collection of props in your classroom in addition to the resources you might include in a role-play area. Older children also love to have the added dimension of a prop or costume, so a special box of props should be considered for all classrooms, not just in KS1. The purpose of these is not for large-scale productions but rather to assist and support children in their improvisations and role-play, or for you to use sometimes when you are taking on a role. The smallest item can help a child's imagination and confidence enormously. Here is a list of suggestions for a starter pack:

- your magic cushion or special chair
- dressing-up clothes
- hats
- telephones

- handbags
- newspapers and magazines
- pots and pans
- plants, ornaments, clock etc.
- supermarket basket
- empty cereal packets, tins, sauce bottles etc.
- tablecloth
- crockery and cutlery
- walking stick and umbrella
- briefcase
- suitcase
- masks
- puppets.

It is also useful to have the following readily available:

- sound effects on your laptop
- recording software on computers
- digital camera
- video camera
- microphone and speakers
- musical instruments
- storage boxes
- hanging rail
- rostra (if space permits).

The last word – a handy hint: car boot sales are an excellent place to find many of these items and others!

The place of drama in primary English

Chapter overview

This chapter aims to help you identify the various places and ways in which drama might fit into your teaching of English. It discusses:

- drama, language and learning
- statutory requirements for drama at Key Stages 1 and 2
- drama as a pedagogical approach
- performance skills and knowledge of theatre arts
- implications for planning
- planning drama for different genres.

Drama, language and learning

English is a core subject in the National Curriculum because it supports and drives our learning, thinking and communication. Language underpins all human activity and behaviour; it is at the heart of life itself. It involves and surrounds us continuously as speech and text; it fills our heads with thoughts; and it is even actively operating when we dream. The most ordinary everyday situations are filled with language. For example: imagine a busy supermarket. There is print everywhere, giving information, instruction, persuasion, explanation and warnings. Now think of all the people in that supermarket who are talking! Different ages, different roles – explaining, complaining, questioning, answering, counting, instructing, and so on. The supermarket is a buzzing hive of forms of language; stop, look and listen next time you are shopping!

The most effective teaching of language and literacy skills is where the learning is set within meaningful contexts that reflect this interactive and dynamic nature of language. Opportunities that enable children to learn English by actually *using* language in practical contexts are essential because they reflect the true nature of language and enable children to participate as active learners rather than passive recipients. Interactive contexts can also have a huge impact on engagement and motivation because most children enjoy this way of learning and improving their practical language skills.

There are three obvious places where drama fits into the teaching of English: first, as a subject in its own right under the requirements for speaking and listening; second, as a pedagogical approach to developing skills, knowledge and understanding across all strands of English; and, third, as a valuable opportunity to learning English through other curriculum subjects. Examples of the third approach are provided throughout this book.

If you are going to plan your teaching to maximise these opportunities for learning English through drama, it is important to know and understand the differences between the explicit statutory requirements and the implicit potential elsewhere. Let us begin with what is required by law at the time of writing.

Statutory requirements for drama at Key Stages 1 and 2

Drama is not a discrete statutory subject in the National Curriculum but within the English requirements it is included explicitly under speaking and listening as follows:

Drama: KS1

To participate in a range of drama activities, pupils should be taught to:

a. use language and actions to explore and convey situations, characters and emotions

b. create and sustain roles individually and when working with others

c. comment constructively on drama they have watched or in which they have taken part.

The range should include:

1. working in role
2. presenting drama and stories to others
3. responding to performances.

(QCA, 1999: page 17)

Here are two examples of activities that would meet these requirements.

Year 1: The role-play area is already established as the Three Bears' Cottage, with relevant props and costumes, and has been used for a few days as such. Now the teacher explains to the children that, while the bears were sleeping, Goldilocks has helped herself to certain items and left a note to say she is running away back to her parents. The children have time to play with this idea, responding to the additional changes the teacher has made to the role-play area. This is further developed as children are encouraged to plan then practise their responses and show these to the rest of the class in role as the three bears.

Year 2: Following a visit from a professional puppet theatre, pupils work in pairs to interview each other in role as a children's television presenter about their responses. This might be structured to give a framework by giving the interviewer question cards or a script. The views and reviews can be presented to the class as a television interview.

Drama KS2

To participate in a wide range of drama activities and to evaluate their own and others' contributions, pupils should be taught to:

a. create, adapt and sustain different roles, individually and in groups

b. use character, action and narrative to convey story, themes, emotions, ideas in plays they devise and script

c. use dramatic techniques to explore characters and issues [for example, hot seating, flashback]

d. evaluate how they and others have contributed to the overall effectiveness of performances.

The range should include:

1. improvisation and working in role

2. scripting and performing in plays

3. responding to performances.

(QCA, 1999: page 23)

Here are two further examples of activities that would meet these requirements.

Year 3: The children visit a theatre to see a puppet company performing a comic play in which actors and puppets interact. After the production the actor/puppeteers explain how they combine performance and puppet manipulation. Back in school, the teacher helps groups of pupils devise short puppet plays for their peers, using some of the performance techniques they have observed.

Year 5: The class has been reading the classic novel *Stig of the Dump* by Clive King (2003). The story is about the adventures experienced by a boy called Barney who discovers a caveman (Stig) living at the bottom of the quarry near his grandmother's house. Paired improvisations of the moment when Barney first falls down into Stig's den can be explored, followed by script writing of the dialogue that emerges. An imagined alternative scenario, to extend thinking beyond the dialogue of the book, could be Stig stumbling into Barney's bedroom.

The inclusion of drama as an explicit requirement goes some way to recognising the valuable part that drama has to play in the intellectual, artistic and social development of primary-aged children. Drama is also referred to within other parts of the National Curriculum, for example in relation to reading (reading and performing plays), and exploring ideas in other subjects such as History and Religious Education. These requirements offer a balanced approach encompassing the experiential and explorative aspects of drama for self-development, described in Chapter 1 in relation to the child-drama movement of the 1960s, and the techniques of performance for others. The two previously polarised foci have been integrated into a common-sense approach requiring different types of drama for different learning objectives. For example, whereas some improvisations may never be repeated, others may be developed and polished into presentations for others. Good primary drama incorporates all the rich and valuable learning to be offered by experiential drama, but also makes space for the performance art-form of drama. Both these approaches are given a clear mandate in the statutory requirements.

However, the specified Order should not be regarded as a restricted band for delivery as this might limit the additional potential of drama to promote English in other ways. With efficient, creative planning and classroom management it is possible to select from a wide range of drama tools to teach English because drama is also a powerful pedagogical approach in its own right.

Drama as a pedagogical approach

Drama can provide the interactive contexts, described at the start of this chapter, that help to make language learning more meaningful for children. Before demonstrating this, let us first consider how closely the strands of English are related. The model in Figure 4.1 illustrates the four strands of primary English: speaking and listening (known together as oracy); reading and writing (known together as literacy). Each sits in its own box, representing the fact that the National Curriculum provides separate learning objectives for each. However, the model also uses arrows to highlight the relationships that might be considered when planning activities: for example, writing then reading a book for younger children, oral evaluation of a peer's writing, reading instructions then explaining them in own words to a group. Integrated approaches to language teaching such as these are an effective way to reinforce many of the skills of language and communication.

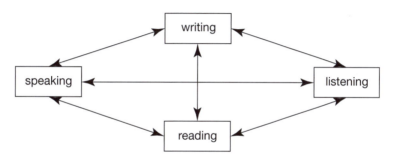

FIGURE 4.1 The integration of language skills.

Drama adds a powerful dimension to language work because it enables children to become active and interactive users. The model in Figure 4.2 illustrates this. This time, the language skills appear in a three-dimensional box, still connected by their arrows, but no longer separated into discrete units. The drama activities, represented in a second box below, generate eight processes:

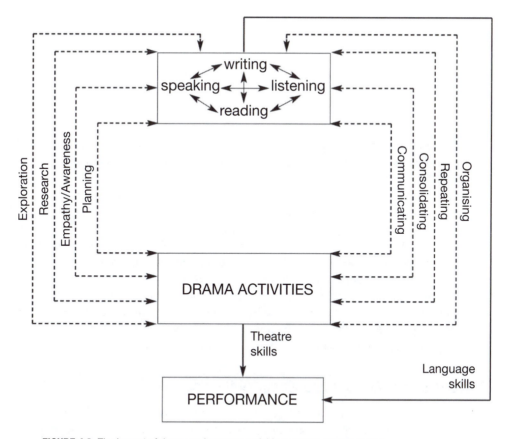

FIGURE 4.2 The impact of drama on language activities: a wrap-around model.

- exploration
- research
- empathy and awareness
- planning
- organising
- repeating
- consolidating
- communicating.

These are all processes (and you can probably add more to the list) that can arise out of the drama, and which set in motion the use of language skills. For instance, an improvisation of conversations between the animals in Anthony Browne's *Zoo* (1994) would aim to generate particular types of talk (e.g. description of feeling, debate about zoos) and could lead to follow-up poetry describing the animals' feelings. The processes can also feed back into the drama (note the two-way arrows); for instance the children might go on to read *Gorilla* by the same author (2008) and discuss the similarities in features, author style and so on. The drama will have particularly helped the children to develop:

- an empathy with the characters
- an awareness of the deeper meanings in the books
- the ability to express the emotions in ways that a simpler discussion might not have produced.

There are two further points to make about this wrap-around model. First, each of the four aspects of English – reading, writing, speaking and listening – can be sub-divided into a multitude of further sub-skills. Imagine the complexity of a model that might attempt to illustrate this; the number of variables operating between all those skills and the eight processes would be countless! With this in mind, it is easy to see that drama offers a wonderful toolbox from which to select when planning your English teaching. Second, the box entitled 'Performance' is in an outlying position at the bottom because it does not always have to be central to the drama. As you continue to read this book, you will learn that performance is not an obligatory outcome of drama, although children do need to be given opportunities to work in this mode from time to time. Sometimes it will be appropriate to communicate their drama in other ways, such as a discussion about how they felt about a simulation once it is over. The communication process arrow represents this in the model.

Performance skills and knowledge of theatre arts

'Sharing' work with others is a common event in primary schools. A dramatic performance is one of the ways that children can show or present their ideas and work. To maximise the potential learning and ensure high standards, this requires particular skills and knowledge of drama as an art form: theatre. Children's 'increasing knowledge and understanding of how the elements of drama work enables them to effectively shape, express and share their ideas, feelings and responses, making use of language, space, symbol, allegory and metaphor' (Arts Council England, 2003: page 4, paragraph 2). This process needs to develop and grow gradually through primary school. For example: if children have been developing a critical awareness through professional theatre visits in and out of school throughout their primary schooling, their own work is going to be inspired and enriched. Alongside this, teachers need to feel confident about providing opportunities for children to explore the creation and construction of theatrical drama. The language and dynamics of theatre provide the tools for children to create and express ideas. A rich and developmental drama curriculum during the primary years can help children to develop the skills and confidence required to do so. The smaller-scale, everyday 'performances', for example presenting ideas in a dramatic form to the rest of the class after a 20-minute activity, make an important contribution to the development of children's knowledge and understanding of theatrical form. A basic overview of more specialised theatre skills and techniques that you may require to extend children's learning further during larger-scale and more public performances is provided in Chapter 9.

Implications for planning

When starting to incorporate drama into your planning for English, you will need to keep three questions firmly in your mind.

- First, how can drama be developed as a discrete subject which enables you to cover the explicit requirements for National Curriculum English and to develop children's awareness and use of drama as an art form?

- Second, how can you use drama to provide purposeful language learning opportunities to promote learning in other aspects of English and other curriculum subjects? This might mean that you 'teach drama' once or twice a week within the first category, whilst also 'using drama as a resource' several times during the week across a range of subject areas.

- Third, how can you differentiate the learning for English? This is explained more fully in Chapter 10.

The relevance of drama is implicit within the four strands of English – speaking, listening, reading and writing. All four are actively interconnected; that is the nature of any language. Drama can enrich the learning and help to develop children's understanding across and between all strands. Table 4.1 gives some examples.

The ideas and examples in subsequent chapters of this book are designed to offer a positive and creative approach to using drama in this way across the four strands of English. These have been separated into discrete chapters in order to highlight the potential for each area of English: reading, writing, speaking and listening. However, inevitably there will always be overlap. For instance, KS1 children might create a puppet performance about 'life when grandma was a girl'. Inspired by a professional performance, they are learning much about the powers of communication in theatre,

TABLE 4.1 Example of drama approaches to facilitate other English learning objectives

LEARNING OBJECTIVE	SUGGESTED DRAMA APPROACH
Express ideas clearly and confidently	Present work in role
Write for a variety of purposes	Writing in role
Prepare and present stories and poems	Performance drama
Read with expression, fluency and accuracy	Use of play scripts as performance texts
Organise information	Present as a radio documentary
Structure talk so it is clear and understandable	News presenters in role
Describe events or experiences	Improvisations in role
Writing dialogue	Writing play scripts

and yet they are also learning about history. Likewise in KS2, you might be using your discrete drama session to explore the theatrical presentation of a point of tension in a reworking of *The Iron Woman* (Hughes, 1993), but there is also valuable learning taking place about characterisation and literature, as required by the statutory programme of study for reading.

Planning drama for different genres

It is also useful to consider how different genres might benefit from appropriate drama activities. Tables 4.2–4.7 provide suggestions for drama activities linking directly into the National Curriculum range of fiction and non-fiction texts. As with all the lists and frameworks in this book, the following planning suggestions are no more than that – suggestions! If you are new to drama, remember to work at a pace that is manageable and enjoyable. But don't hold back! Using drama with your pupils will bring you many rich rewards, and provide your children with learning opportunities that they will never forget.

TABLE 4.2 Drama planning for English: Reception and Year 1

	TERM 1	TERM 2	TERM 3
Fiction and poetry	Stories with familiar settings; stories and rhymes with predictable and repetitive patterns	Traditional stories and rhymes; fairy stories; stories with familiar, predictable and patterned language from a range of cultures, including playground chants, action verses and rhymes; plays	Stories about fantasy worlds, poems with patterned and predictable structures; a variety of poems on similar themes
Non-fiction	Signs, labels, captions, lists, instructions	Information books, including non-chronological reports, simple dictionaries	Information texts including recounts of observation, visits, events
Drama activities	<ul><li>Office role-play area</li><li>Writing lists in role as characters from stories</li><li>Writing lists for teacher who is in role as forgetful character</li><li>Teacher in role as story character to answer questions in the hot seat</li><li>Whole-class improvisation following instructions on flipchart sheet (giant letter) journey through a magic forest</li></ul>	<ul><li>Library role-play area</li><li>Miming fairy-tale characters</li><li>Improvisation changing endings of familiar stories</li><li>Re-enacting stories with puppets as a play activity</li><li>Changing the stories using puppets</li><li>Re-enacting stories using masks</li></ul>	<ul><li>Travel agent role-play area</li><li>Guided action through fantasy world</li><li>Puppet actions to poems</li><li>Puppet actions to children's own poems</li><li>Dynamic duos, questioning about a visit (in role) prior to writing</li><li>Re-enacting an event prior to writing</li></ul>

TABLE 4.3 Drama planning for English: Year 2

	TERM 1	TERM 2	TERM 3
Fiction and poetry	Stories and a variety of poems with familiar settings	Traditional stories: stories and poems from other cultures; stories and poems with predictable and patterned language; poems by significant children's poets	Extended stories: stories by significant children's authors; different stories by the same author; texts with language play
Non-fiction	Instructions	Dictionaries, glossaries, indexes and other alphabetically ordered texts Explanations	Information books including non-chronological reports
Drama activities	• Pantomime role-play area • Telling stories to mimed actions • Improvisations and retelling the event • Writing instructions in role • Detached voices giving instructions to mime • Explore character motivation through hot seating	• Tourist information role-play area • Improvising endings from unfinished stories/comparing with actual ending • Dynamic duos to explain a misdemeanour • Dynamic duo interviews to discuss favourite story, poem or author • Simulation of celebrations from other cultures	• School role-play area • Research from non-fiction to create scenes/report live (non-chronologically) • Create mini-documentaries on area of interest (to encourage non-chronological approach) • Teacher hot seating as expert in an area/children ask questions, teacher models non-chronological reporting

TABLE 4.4 Drama planning for English: Year 3

	TERM 1	TERM 2	TERM 3
Fiction and poetry	Stories with familiar settings; plays; poems based on observation and the senses; shape poems	Myths, legends, fables, parables; traditional stories, stories with related themes; oral and performance poetry from different cultures	Adventure and mystery stories; stories by the same author; humorous poetry, poetry that plays with language, word puzzles, puns, riddles
Non-fiction	Information books on topics of interest Non-chronological reports Thesauruses, dictionaries	Instructions Dictionaries without illustrations, thesauruses	Letters written for a range of purposes; to recount, explain, enquire, complain, congratulate etc. Alphabetic texts, directories, encyclopaedias, indexes, etc.
Drama activities	• Publishers' role-play area • Dance-drama on the senses • Tableaux based on observations/link with follow-up poetry or vice versa • Victorian schoolroom simulation, practising handwriting • In role planning a large building programme (brainstorming, leaflets, posters etc.)	• Role-play area on historical theme • Play reading • Play blocking • Reconstructed improvisations into play scripts/groups exchange scripts • Writing stage directions • Simulated events from other cultures	• 'Science lab' role-play area (white coats, safe materials, forms, documents, reports, books etc.) • Guided action through mysterious landscapes • Guided imagery to explore strange environments • Making mystery plays for the radio reading and writing letters in role

TABLE 4.5 Drama planning for English: Year 4

	TERM 1	TERM 2	TERM 3
Fiction and poetry	Historical stories and short novels; play scripts; poems based on common themes, e.g. space, school, animals, families, feelings, viewpoints	Stories/novels about imagined worlds; sci-fi, fantasy adventures; stories in series; classic and modern poetry, including poems from different cultures and times	Stories/short novels that raise issues, e.g. bullying, bereavement, injustice; stories by same author; stories from other cultures. Range of poetry in different forms
Non-fiction	A range of text types from reports and articles in newspapers and magazines etc.; instructions	Information books on same or similar themes Explanation	Persuasive writing: adverts, circulars, flyers Discussion texts: debates, editorials Information books linked to other curricular areas
Drama activities	<ul><li>Role-play area on theme from a story</li><li>Improvisations on family issues</li><li>Character documentaries</li><li>Tableaux on feelings</li><li>Tableaux on feelings with detached voices</li><li>Newspaper stories: improvise story and parts not reported</li><li>Interviews for magazines</li></ul>	<ul><li>Space station role-play area</li><li>Performances of poems from other cultures</li><li>Researching for tableaux</li><li>Researching to create and present TV</li><li>Documentary</li><li>Spontaneous improvisation in pairs on explanation</li><li>Child in hot seat to explain (under attack!)</li></ul>	<ul><li>Role-play area with another cultural theme</li><li>Tableaux on issues/ bring alive the tableaux</li><li>Paired improvisations on issues</li><li>Poetry presentations with music and sound effects</li><li>Designing adverts, circulars, flyers in role for specific purpose (e.g. new leisure centre)</li><li>Simulated meeting to debate hot issue</li></ul>

TABLE 4.6 Drama planning for English: Year 5

	TERM 1	TERM 2	TERM 3
Fiction and poetry	Novels, stories and poems by significant children's writers Play scripts Concrete poetry	Traditional stories, myths, legends and fables from a range of cultures Longer classic poetry, including narrative poetry	Novels, stories and poems from a variety of cultures and traditions; choral and performance poetry
Non-fiction	Recounting of events, activities, visits; observation records, news reports etc. Instructional texts: rules, recipes, directions, etc. showing how things are done	Non-chronological reports (i.e. to describe and classify) Explanations (processes, systems, operations etc.) Use content from other subjects	Persuasive writing to put or argue a point of view: letters, commentaries, leaflets to persuade, criticise, protest, support, object, complain Dictionaries, thesauruses, including IT sources
Drama activities	• Hotel kitchen role-play area • News programme with live reports and summaries • Poetry as theme for improvisations • Enacting plays from scripts • Writing additional stage directions to play scripts	• Role-play area on theme of myth or legend working with extracts from more advanced plays • Longer exploration of narrative poem (e.g. *Pied Piper, Ancient Mariner*) • Perform extracts from myths, others watch as if reporters on the scene, and make notes • Puppet theatre of myths and legends	• Office role-play area with ICT • Performance of poetry with narrative action • Writing letters in role following a relevant improvisation or simulation • Exploring the use of masks in drama • Telephone calls in dynamic duos to protest or criticise

TABLE 4.7 Drama planning for English: Year 6

	TERM 1	TERM 2	TERM 3
Fiction and poetry	Classic fiction, poetry and drama by long-established authors including, where appropriate, study of a Shakespeare play; adaptations of classics on film/TV	Longer established stories and novels selected from more than one genre; e.g. mystery, humour, sci-fi, historical, fantasy worlds etc. to study and compare; range of poetic forms	Comparison of work by significant children's author(s) and poets: work by same author; different authors' treatment of same theme(s)
Non-fiction	Autobiography and biography, diaries, journals, letters, anecdotes, records of observations etc. which recount experience and events Journalistic writing; non-chronological reports	Discussion texts; texts which set out a point of view Formal writing: notices, public information documents	Explanations linked to work from other subjects Non-chronological reports linked to work from other subjects Reference texts, range of dictionaries, thesauruses, including IT sources
Drama activities	▪ TV studio role-play area ▪ Presentation of *Newsnight* specials on a theme ▪ Retelling of *Macbeth* with mime alongside puppet versions of *Macbeth* ▪ Contemporary improvisations of *Macbeth* characters	▪ Futuristic role-play area ▪ Improvisations and simulations to provoke public debate ▪ Retelling of *The Tempest* ▪ Puppet versions of *The Tempest* ▪ Interviews with Prospero and Miranda ▪ Writing in role ▪ Reading in role	▪ Theatre role-play area with various costumes and props ▪ Hot seating characters and authors ▪ Retelling of *A Midsummer Night's Dream* ▪ Mini performances of *Pyramus and Thisbe* ▪ Shortened version of *A Midsummer Night's Dream*

Developing speaking and listening skills

Chapter overview

This chapter aims to provide an overview of how drama can be used to help children learn about and develop their speaking and listening skills. It discusses:

- speaking, listening and learning
- speaking and listening in the primary curriculum
- speaking, listening and drama
- the range of talk
- providing an audience for children's talk
- listening and responding
- Standard English and language study
- speaking, listening and literacy.

Speaking, listening and learning

Speaking and listening are sometimes referred to collectively as 'oracy' in the same way that 'literacy' is used to describe reading and writing. Spoken language is central to human communication. Not only does it make meaning through words and syntactical structures, it also creates further meaning through other dynamics: tone, volume, expression, accent, speed and body language. Text can seem two-dimensional in comparison with the spoken word, even though one is derived directly from the other. Children need to develop into confident talkers so they can express themselves clearly and confidently when communicating for a range of purposes. They need these skills not only to equip them for their future lives, but also to operate as learners during their schooling. The development of speaking and listening skills in the primary school goes far beyond merely learning how to speak proficiently. It plays a vital role in supporting children's wider progress in thinking, learning and communication, and, in particular, has a significant impact on the development of their reading and writing skills.

An increasing number of children are starting school with impoverished language skills, and yet the Bercow Report (2008) identified a significant lack of understanding by policy-makers and professionals of the centrality of speech, language and communication to children's learning and development. It is important, therefore, that primary teachers recognise the important part that oracy has to play in children's schooling, and in particular the impact that their teaching of speaking and listening can have on all aspects of children's language. Speaking and listening should not be regarded as a disconnected strand within the English curriculum, taught only because it is a requirement to do so. Recognising the significance of oracy has to start with an understanding of the complex ways that children learn to talk, and the importance of interaction in the classroom.

Early language learning

The various well-established theories about how children actually learn to talk have one thing in common: the essential influence of interaction with others on the rates of development. Children do not learn to talk in isolation. They talk by hearing adults and other children modelling a wide range of talk patterns, by repeating and experimenting with making sounds, by learning from others' responses to their sounds and adapting or practising them, often during their play. In other words, oracy is a dynamic, social and interactive process. Research has shown that children from privileged home backgrounds with abundant and varied opportunities for talk have a significantly larger vocabulary by the time they are three years old than children from impoverished backgrounds where interaction is more limited (Wells, 1986; Hart and Risley, 2003). Not only is the word deficit limiting in itself, it also restricts thought construction, conceptual understanding and the ability to create more advanced spoken and written linguistic structures.

Vygotsky's social-psycholinguistic theory (1978) continues to demonstrate how young children use speech to organise their thinking, particularly when problem-solving. This theory has stood the test of time; the running commentaries that we observe children making as they play are clear examples of externalised thought, and there is much evidence to show that this is helpfully guiding the learning process (Berk, 1994). The early work of Bruner (1986) likewise explored the use of language as a tool for learning and in particular the importance of talk to assist understanding. This is easily understood when one considers the stream of questions that young children constantly ask as they explore and find out about their world!

From home to school

Once children start school, the scope for developing spoken language does not necessarily increase, whatever the ability of the child. Indeed, progress might actually slow down for some children when they start school if the language environment is restrictive or alien to them (Wells, 1986). In the case of children with more advanced oracy skills, progress can slow down if they are channelled into unnaturally passive roles in which they must sustain long periods of silence. This can prevent their natural curiosity, which is such a crucial contributory factor in learning development. Furthermore, to undermine the linguistic confidence and self-concept of young children by trying to modify their accent or criticising the language of the home can also inhibit and threaten their self-esteem and inhibit their motivation. Both these aspects are well recognised and addressed by the statutory early years curriculum, which promotes active learning, wide opportunities for speaking and listening, and positive respect for and engagement with each child's home and individuality.

The cultural contexts of children's homes and the varied range of experiences will have resulted in very different individual learning needs that should also be recognised. Teachers should take an obvious interest in the life of the child beyond school. The variation in the language of families across Britain is enormous. Not only are there cultural differences resulting from the rich ethnic diversity of our society, but there is also a multitude of dialects even within tight geographical areas. Language is laden with value systems, and carries many implicit meanings in addition to the literal meanings of words. These can occasionally be the subject of prejudice and stereotyping, which, in a classroom situation, can be very damaging to a child's confidence.

It has been argued that children whose language is closest to that of the teacher and the culture of the school are at an advantage when starting school. They are used to the linguistic structures and vocabulary, they know and use many of the social conventions, they are comfortable with the accents, and communication is therefore effective because it is a continuation of that which is familiar and in which the child has developed competence at home. On the other hand, children who bring to school a community dialect that includes relatively little Standard English, or those whose first language is not the first language of the school, are faced with more challenges. For an increasing number of children, considerable enhancement and enrichment is required: for example, where the home has not provided experiences such as listening to and talking about stories.

The good practice that is commonly found in early years settings in promoting speaking and listening is not always carried forward when children enter the more formal schooling in KS1. Schools should also ask how children's oracy is nurtured and developed through KS2. How can teachers provide a learning environment where children continue to learn and think with the help of their private speech and shared talk? Oracy throughout the primary curriculum should be designed in such a way that children can learn *through* speaking and listening, but also learn *about* speaking and listening in order to continue developing new skills and understanding. This should enable them to communicate with an ever-widening range of audiences for an ever-widening range of purposes.

Speaking and listening in the primary curriculum

As children progress through the school system, the focus on oracy tends to reduce. Curriculum subjects become increasingly compartmentalised and content-based, and passive modes of learning take over from participatory interactive learning.

Pedagogically, this can be a mistake. This has been recognised at the highest levels based on extensive evidence. For example, the Bercow Report (2008) recommended that speech, language and communication should be a core requirement of the curriculum and that teacher training should reflect this.

The National Curriculum for English has included a statutory requirement for speaking and listening since 1988 and yet, all too often, it is not sufficiently prioritised by schools. It is vital that teachers continue to plan for speaking and listening just as thoroughly as they do for reading and writing. Drama can be a significant part of that planning, both as a discrete area with content of its own and as a means of providing meaningful contexts for other oracy activities.

Speaking, listening and drama

A rigorous review of the primary curriculum (Rose, 2009) acknowledged that drama has a valuable part to play in the development of children's speaking and listening:

> Although all subjects have potential for developing spoken language, some are particularly valuable in this respect. For example, the appeal to primary children of role play, and drama in its various forms, is often used very successfully to develop speaking and listening and leads to other worthy outcomes.
>
> (page 72)

Drama is included in the National Curriculum requirements for Speaking and Listening. In KS1, pupils should be encouraged to participate in drama activities, improvisation and performances of varying kinds, using language appropriate to a role or situation. They should be given opportunities to respond to drama they have watched, as well as that in which they have participated. In KS2, pupils should be given opportunities to participate in a wide range of drama activities, including improvisation, role-play, and the writing and performance of scripted drama. In responding to drama, they should be encouraged to evaluate their own and others' contributions. As explained in Chapter 4, drama also has a valuable part to play as the mode of delivery for promoting other aspects of English. Drama can facilitate a whole range of purposes for which speaking might be needed by offering roles, situations, contexts and a variety of approaches to setting these up. In drama, pupils can learn to *use* talk, and they can also learn *about* talk. Involvement and interaction are crucial components of the development of talk; drama can offer both these things!

The range of talk

The interactive and dynamic nature of speaking and listening means that we talk for many different reasons and purposes. For example, the last hour of work, the journey home, a meal with the family and a night out with a best friend would all be likely to involve different reasons for talking: *explaining* something to a colleague, *asking* the garage attendant why the petrol pump isn't working properly, *complaining* to your partner that it's beans on toast again, and *relating* a piece of news to your friend. It is important that pupils develop an understanding of this concept of range, and are provided with opportunities to talk for a wide variety of purposes just as we do in life. Drama enables you to set up situations so that children can experience many different contexts, roles and relationships. For example:

- telling stories
- predicting outcomes
- giving reasons for actions
- describing events.

Drama has an obvious part to play in providing the mechanisms for such types of talk and many others. So, when planning talk activities it is important to be guided by types of talk as well as the purpose. 'Sharing ideas' is a *purpose*, but for that purpose we could use various *types of talk* such as recalling, predicting, describing, suggesting, listing and so on. Planning to ensure that the children are *learning about* different types of talk and *using* different types of talk requires good teacher knowledge of the options available. Table 5.1 shows two lists of talk types: *concrete talk*, in which the talk tends to be supported by actual experience such as an event, a resource, an observation and so on; and *abstract talk*, which is based more on thoughts and ideas. This is not a definitive list, and there is an inevitable overlapping of categories (for instance, planning might draw on recapping, sequencing and explaining). However, they have been divided in order to help you reflect more analytically about how different types of talk require different skills and levels of knowledge.

When engaging in concrete talk, the children would usually have subject matter upon which to base their talk, whereas abstract talk relies more heavily on thoughts

TABLE 5.1 Types of talk

CONCRETE TALK	ABSTRACT TALK
Based upon prior event, observation, knowledge etc.	Based on thought, ideas, indirect experience etc.
• retelling (story, poem, news)	• planning
• relating (messages)	• predicting
• reporting (event, results, findings)	• suggesting ideas
• reflecting (on what has happened before)	• developing ideas
• responding	• investigating
• giving instructions	• imagined stories
• explaining (choice, decision, action)	• persuading
• asking a question	• expressing opinion
• answering a question	• qualifying an argument
• listing	• expressing insights
• sequencing	
• describing	
• evaluating	
• commenting	
• justifying	
• reasoned argument	

and ideas. Having said that, drama generally requires children to imagine and so they might be using concrete talk whilst applying imaginative and developmental skills. Arguably, this could be a further reason to justify using drama because it provides 'surrogate' subject matter for the development of abstract thought.

Table 5.2 provides some examples of how a type of talk might lead the drama; in other words, having decided which type of talk you wish the children to engage in, a drama activity can be designed in order to provide that opportunity.

Providing an audience for children's talk

Talk routinely requires something to talk about and someone to talk to! We speak differently according to our audience: more formally to some than to others. Even those we know well can unknowingly demand different styles: for example speaking to a parent, a sibling and a friend might result in different tone and vocabulary, speaking to a friend of one gender might be different from speaking to a friend of the other gender, and so on. The National Curriculum makes specific reference to audience for speaking and listening, requiring children to identify the needs of different audiences and speak in ways that address those needs.

Providing different audiences helps to motivate the children because it gives the activity a purpose and a focus. The audience in question might be 'real', for example other groups, the whole class, other classes, parents and carers, or visitors. Alternatively, drama can provide any other audience you care to imagine by putting the children in role. In other words, the drama can provide 'pretend audiences' as well as 'pretend speakers'!

TABLE 5.2 Talk types in drama contexts

TALK TYPE	DRAMA CONTEXT
Reporting	KS1: school role-play, teacher reporting on pupils' performance KS2: role-play in pairs, reporting a burglary in a shopping centre
Explaining	KS1: explaining to Goldilocks why she was rude to invade the three bears' house KS2: in role as historical character, explaining a trade or event
Asking questions	KS1: travel agents' role-play area/taking bookings KS2: role-play interviews in pairs
Predicting	KS1: spontaneous improvisation, exploring a secret castle, predicting what they might find KS2: group presentation of a famous scientific discovery
Investigating	KS1: following clues (which you have written and hidden) in the home corner KS2: documentary on an investigation into bullying
Expressing opinion	KS1: about a play they have been to see at the theatre KS2: role-play of two opposing politicians talking about banning parking in cities

Audience in role

Imagine that you want the children to explain their activities at school, paying attention to description and justification. Ask them to plan a presentation in groups, imagining that they are the teachers of a school. The headteacher has invited all the new parents and carers to a meeting at the start of the school year to give them information about the school. As each group 'performs' their prepared presentation in role, the rest of the children will also be in role as the visiting parents and carers. They will listen critically so that they can ask questions (in role as parents and carers). This not only serves the purpose of focusing the minds of the presenters on their target audience but also creates an added dimension to the process of hearing– a more participatory involvement than simply listening passively. The 'audience in role' approach also offers the chance for peer evaluation and giving feedback to each other about how they spoke and how they listened. Questions such as 'How did the teachers use their voices when they were explaining?' or 'Did they answer the questions clearly?' can add useful teaching opportunities about the use of language. The list in Table 5.3 shows some other examples of how the children could provide specific audiences in role.

Audiences can come in different sizes, and it is worth referring to Chapter 4 to see how children can be grouped in different ways for different purposes relating to the 'audience in role' approach.

Listening and responding

Listening is an integral part of oracy, and there are clear expectations within the National Curriculum about how children should use and develop their listening skills. However, listening is difficult to monitor and assess, because it is not as observable as we sometimes assume. The well-worn exhortation 'I want you to listen quietly!' belies the true complexity of listening skills. Children might be still and quiet, but how can you know that they are listening? They might be miles away, dreaming about a forthcoming birthday party! It can be helpful to ask yourself what you expect from

TABLE 5.3 Creating audiences through drama

ACTIVITY	AUDIENCE ROLE
Home corner role-play	Teacher as neighbour calling in for cup of tea
Police interviews	Pupil in role as police requiring a clear description
Documentary programme	Class as TV critics
Teacher operating hand puppets	Pupils asking the puppets questions
Group story performance	Other groups guessing the moral of the story
Explaining electricity	Tudor time travellers
Describing an earthquake	News reporters at a press conference
Giving instructions about a picnic event	Teddy bears

their listening. There are two main outcomes that should be required from listening, understanding and response, and the two are closely linked.

Understanding leads to extension or adaptation of knowledge and concepts. If children listen with understanding, they are more likely to remember what they have heard. In turn, they can respond, which helps them to assimilate further and use that knowledge in transferable ways. Responses come in many shapes and sizes: following instructions, answering questions, retelling, disagreeing, making relevant comment and so on.

In order to assess children's listening skills, you need to be clear about the expected outcomes that you believe provide evidence of understanding and/or response. This is discussed in relation to assessment in Chapter 10, but here are some questions that you might ask during drama activities to ascertain the quality of the listening:

- *Police interview:* are they asking questions that build on the evidence given?
- *Public debate:* are they using the arguments of others to make a case against the opposition?
- *Watching a group performance:* can they compare and contrast two types of talk?
- *Role-play area:* can they follow three separate instructions in sequence?

When setting up listening activities, the quality of the listening will depend to a great extent on the interest and quality of the talk. It is human nature to switch off when we are bored! This is another reason why drama can be a useful tool: it can bring the activity 'alive', adding to it a compelling desire to listen. However, you also need to make it clear to the children that you have expectations of their listening, for example 'As we continue with the public meeting I am going to make notes on how you use other people's arguments to build up your own points' or 'As we make our journey together across the desert island, I am going to give you clues about who I am, which I will ask you to remember at the end when we get back to the classroom.'

Watching the drama of others, whether it be other groups in the class or a professional performance, enables children to create new knowledge and theorise about that knowledge. Discussing, analysing and interpreting will help children with the process of assimilating the experience.

Standard English and language study

Language is complex and interesting to study. It is constantly changing, a living, breathing, developing phenomenon. Standard English is only one of many forms of language construction or dialects. It is the central 'rule book' form as taught to speakers of other languages. It is also used where a commonly agreed format is required to enable all participants to understand each other clearly: for example, in business, media, politics and international affairs. This does not mean that other dialects are inferior; they are simply different. Regional dialects are community-based, specific to particular geographic areas, and therefore do not necessarily have all the common features required for wider communication. However, the rich variation of sounds, structures and vocabulary that can be found around Britain is interesting and colourful, and should be seen as part of our cultural heritage rather than something that should be homogenised into a unified form.

Certain linguistic features can also be specific to age groups; for example some 'teenage words and phrases' transcend all geographical divisions, and yet are rarely used by other generations. To further complicate matters, this changes from decade to decade. The vocabulary of teenagers in the 1960s (e.g. 'groovy', 'fab' and 'flower power') was very different from that of young people today (e.g. 'cool', 'well bad' and 'sorted')! The adaptations of words and the development of new words, not just by teenagers, are processes that have taken place continuously through history. One only has to compare texts from Chaucer, Shakespeare and Austen to see examples of this, along with all the Eurospeak and information technology vocabulary that has flooded the English language since the start of the twenty-first century. Language changes, grows and adapts, and this can be a fascinating subject to explore with children as a means of teaching them to be informed users.

Language also has powerful social connotations of power, status and worth. Stereotyping according to accent or dialect is still a common feature of British society. As teachers we should be extremely careful not to alienate children, or threaten their self-esteem, by dismantling the language that is part of their identity. Dialect is an important part of many children's lives because it has been central to their language and learning prior to starting school, and continues to be central to their lives at home and in their communities alongside the language of school.

Nevertheless, if children are to have equal opportunities in a society where different dialects, including Standard English, are required for different purposes and audiences, then it is vital that we provide them with the multilingual skills to switch from one to another and the knowledge of when and why it is appropriate to do so. Using linguistic variation through drama can make it possible to present a range of language scenarios in order to motivate children to learn about language whilst at the same time developing their user skills in different situations.

Examples of such activities might include:

- writing dialect poems and raps for performance
- looking at and performing dialect from stories and poems
- recording radio adverts with different accents
- using regional words in drama (e.g. bread roll, bap, batch, cob, flour cake)
- transcribing dialect from soap operas into Standard English and performing both versions
- translation of parts of the drama by speakers of other languages
- writing alternative scripts of talk for different purposes
- comparing the grammar of spoken forms arising from improvisations with written forms: script versus a report of the scene
- discussing the differences between boys' talk and girls' talk during a class improvisation where the pupils change gender roles
- rehearsing formal situations such as job interviews.

Providing models for talk

Just as children's early language development relies upon exposure to and interaction with other people speaking, so is it necessary to hear different examples of speech if they are to learn a range of approaches to language. Different types of talk require different constructions and vocabulary: for example, predicting normally uses the future tense whereas reporting uses the past. If children are going to learn to use features of Standard English for particular purposes, they need to hear good examples upon which they can model their own attempts. Modelling can be provided by recordings, DVDs, visitors and most of all you. Drama enables children to use the language, and interact with you in role while you model the language you are teaching. Here are some examples:

- *Planning a camping trip: use of future tense.* 'What are we going to take with us? I am going to take a warm sleeping bag. What are you going to take, Deepak?'

- *Reporting what happened during a midnight visit to Santa's workshop: use of past tense.* 'So what happened next, Leanne? Oh, you found a pile of empty sacks. I wonder why they were empty? What did you find, Sofia? You found a kettle that was still warm? What did you think about that?'

- *Interview with headteacher about an incident: use of conjunctions.* 'So you threw the ball outside the gates because you were cross with Carl. Did you tell anyone before you climbed over the wall?'

You will notice from these examples that modelling includes repeating back to the child the correct version, so that they are hearing it more than once as well as saying it themselves.

Extending vocabulary

If children are provided with situations that require new vocabulary they will also need preparation and resources to help them access that vocabulary as well as building on the models you provide in your own language. This might come from a range of places such as:

- introductory explanations
- hearing texts read aloud
- researching from texts
- recording on CDs and DVDs
- labels on the wall
- game cards.

The drama can be constructed in ways that will require the children to use the vocabulary; for example words such as 'conflict', 'debate', 'decision' and 'finalise' could be focus words used during a public meeting. Or when reporting an event, rather than stringing together their ideas with 'and then' children could be encouraged to use other conjunctions by using conjunction cue cards (large flash cards each with a conjunction on them: after/since/whenever/although/because/except that etc.). Each time they use a card they score a point, so the drama in this context is more of a language game.

Although it may not always be appropriate to 'interrupt' the drama, you should take every opportunity you can to make explicit the points you are aiming to teach. This is usually done most successfully by acknowledgement and specific praise.

Speaking clearly and confidently

Clarity is something that can be modelled for children, but which they also need to practise. Clarity requires appropriate speed and volume. It also requires expression that helps the meaning, and logical organisation where a sequence of ideas is being expressed. Clarity is about successfully 'reaching' your audience.

There is a world of difference between forcing children to alter their natural speech as 'themselves' and asking them to do this in role. Working in role can assist learning in the following ways.

- It protects self-esteem by de-personalising a process which is, in reality, an extremely personal and sensitive part of a child's self-perception.
- It provides enjoyable reasons for speaking 'differently'.
- It offers the disguise or mask of someone different in which to experiment.
- It enables you to correct the 'character' rather than the child.
- It helps children to understand diversity as opposed to one 'wrong way' of speaking and one 'correct way' of speaking.
- It provides a context for repetition, practice and preparation.

Children who lack confidence in their own speech can often be nurtured by working in role. As they become more confident with this, they can gradually transfer skills such as presenting, explaining, and debating to speaking activities that relate to their own personal work.

Speaking, listening and literacy

The teaching of literacy should be underpinned by speaking and listening. Opportunities to discuss, express and explore ideas orally prior to writing are essential. Drama is an invaluable tool to use as part of literacy teaching. Even when the key learning objectives relate to reading or writing, the learning is deeper and longer-lasting when the learning process involves talk. With judicious and creative planning, drama can help you construct the oral elements of literacy learning because it enables you to:

- model language in role
- provide opportunities for children to explore and discuss language in role

- use texts as starting points for exploration
- link reading and writing in meaningful contexts
- play language games for repetition and consolidation
- define changes of pace and focus (e.g. teacher in role/questions/writing follow-up/performance/evaluation and feedback).

If children are working on texts, this should not mean labouring through dry de-contextualised exercises for six consecutive years! Children will learn more effectively about literacy at word, sentence and text level if they *talk* about and *use* those texts prior to writing. The growth of a child's confidence will depend to a very large extent upon your attitudes and the ethos you create in your classroom. An oracy environment that is supportive, active and interesting is going to be more effective than one which is critical, didactic and restrictive. Modelling and praise are powerful tools, as we see when babies imitate sounds and then repeat them in response to the attention poured upon them for doing so! Expectations should be clear and realistic. Progression should be developmental and satisfying. Drama enables all these things to happen, and should constitute a significant part of every school's schemes of work for speaking and listening.

Creating contexts for writing

Chapter overview

This chapter aims to provide an overview of how drama can be used to help children learn about and develop their writing skills. It discusses:

- writing in the primary school

- using drama as writing develops

- how drama can help children to write

- fiction, non-fiction and poetry

- providing responses to children's writing

- useful resources for drama and writing.

Writing in the primary school

Once upon a time, the most common approach to teaching writing for primary school pupils was so-called 'one-shot' writing. From the children's point of view, the main purpose of the writing was so that it could be marked, and therefore the only perceived audience was the teacher. The genre would usually be 'news' from the weekend (recount) on a Monday and a story (narrative) later in the week. A title would be given, the story written in one draft, collected, marked and returned to the child the following week. It has since been acknowledged that this approach to writing is limited in terms of teaching children to understand the wider uses for writing.

Similarly, redrafting is now seen as a valuable part of the learning process, where appropriate. Professional writers tend not to complete a final copy at first sitting! The planning, writing, editing, proofreading, redrafting and final checks are all important parts of the writing process, involving different reading and writing skills. Not all of these stages are needed for every piece of writing, and learning when and when not to apply them is part of understanding the writing process. Different forms or genres of writing require different processing.

There has been a significant move towards broadening the variety of genres in which children are required to write. In the real world, adults do not just write stories. Indeed, many adults do not write stories at all! If you stop to think about how many writing activities you have engaged in during the last week, you will see that you have probably applied your writing skills in a range of ways: filling in forms, shopping lists, letters, notes, messages on birthday cards, email, texts, resource cards for school, report forms and so on. These written forms were probably intended for different readers: your partner, a double glazing company, parents and carers at school and so on. It is therefore desirable that children should develop an understanding of:

- writing for a range of purposes (e.g. to instruct, amuse, remind etc.)
- writing in a range of structures (e.g. note form, list, poem etc.)
- writing for a range of readers (e.g. other children, TV producers, politicians etc.).

Spelling, handwriting, punctuation and grammar are the basic tools of writing, and it is essential that these be taught and assessed systematically and rigorously. However, if children are taught to use these tools in meaningless and detached ways, they are not going to make the conceptual connections between skills and function. Writing should be enjoyable and purposeful if children are going to develop into motivated and independent writers. Setting writing activities into a variety of contexts can help them to learn about writing more effectively and will also sustain their interest.

When they start school, most children already have a considerable amount of implicit knowledge about the writing process. Inevitably, they will emulate what they see around. The purposes for which they choose to write will reflect the models to which they have been exposed. Children imitate what they see around them in their play, and this constitutes a significant part of their learning. We live in a world that is immersed in print that extends beyond simply books: food packets, bill boards and posters in streets, text on television, mobile phones, the Internet, daily post, newspapers, magazines, leaflets. Young children can learn from these that:

- print carries messages and meaning
- those messages can be spoken out loud
- print is represented by symbols
- print is different from pictures
- they can interact with print, particularly through technology.

In school, we set about the business of making children's knowledge explicit, in other words, helping them to become aware of what they know so that new knowledge can be built on those foundations. We should never underestimate the importance of early concepts about print, because to teach without them is like building a house on sand. As their knowledge and experiences of print grow, young children develop new understanding such as directionality, the differences between letters and words, letter formation, and how letter sounds relate to shapes.

Learning to write is developmental, so to force children into formal and meaning-less exercises with no regard for current levels of conceptual understanding can waste time and lead to frustration and even fear of writing. It is therefore important for you to have a clear overview of how children's writing develops as they progress through primary school. Regardless of the age you teach, there will be children in your class who will be at different stages along the developmental continuum. Clearly, there is a wealth of detailed information for teachers on the subject of the developmental stages in writing and it is beyond the scope of this book to provide the finer detail. Nevertheless, it is useful to look here at how the application of drama to learning writing might link in to children's development.

Using drama as writing develops

A particularly useful model for the development of writing, originally researched and developed by the Education Department of Western Australia (Raison, 1994), contin-ues to provide a highly effective continuum as part of the wider language programme known as *First Steps* (EDWA, 1997). This programme identifies clusters of 'key indica-tors' that describe certain writing behaviours typical of each stage. These are offered as an alternative to a linear sequence, as children tend to exhibit certain groups of behaviours within each stage, and are not necessarily sequential. The phases of writing development established by this research are:

Phase 1   Role-play writing

Phase 2   Experimental writing

Phase 3   Early writing

Phase 4   Conventional writing

Phase 5   Proficient writing

Phase 6   Advanced writing.

Another framework, developed with trainee teachers at Oxford Brookes University (Clipson-Boyles, 2010), is used in Table 6.1 to demonstrate how drama might support children's writing at different stages of their development.

How drama can help children to write

Teachers have become highly skilled in formulating writing activities that give chil-dren 'real reasons' for writing. Drama is an invaluable tool for providing contexts that not only motivate children to write but can also assist their understanding of the needs of the reader. Just as there are many approaches to teaching drama, as described in Chapter 2, so are there many ways in which writing activities can be linked to, or stimulated by, the drama. During your daily teaching of literacy, you can and should include drama when appropriate. Drama helps to bring meaning to the language work you are teaching, and can provide multiple contexts for working with the range of texts required by the National Curriculum. This does not necessarily mean that the

TABLE 6.1 Drama activities for the developmental stages of writing

PHASE	CHARACTERISTICS	REQUIREMENTS OF THE DRAMA
Stage 1: The Emergent Writer	▪ knows that print carries meaning ▪ writes for different purposes as part of play activities ▪ discriminates between writing and drawing ▪ writes some letters and similar shapes	To role-play reading activities, and start to focus on writing and saying words during the play
Stage 2: The Exploratory Writer	▪ understands link between sounds and symbols ▪ invents spellings based on that understanding ▪ leaves spaces between words ▪ perceives self as a writer and reads own writing aloud ▪ understands directionality	To write for others who will read their texts as part of the play To use other resources containing texts as part of the play To focus on concepts of sentence
Stage 3: The Communicative Writer	▪ writes texts that can be read by others ▪ seeks information from range of sources (e.g. letters from books, posters, labels) ▪ understands sentence units ▪ will sometimes correct or edit work after reading through	To work with a range of formats for different purposes
Stage 4: The Reflective Writer	▪ adapts style according to purpose and audience ▪ checks, reconsiders and redrafts own work ▪ recognises the need for correct punctuation, spelling and grammar ▪ evaluates the communicative effectiveness of own writing	To study real texts and model writing techniques in role, including editing, proofreading and producing texts for final publication
Stage 5: The Versatile Writer	▪ adapts style according to purpose and audience ▪ moves text around to reorganise ideas ▪ uses ambitious vocabulary ▪ uses complex sentence structures	To provide contexts that will extend the boundaries of reasons to write, requiring more challenging styles, frameworks and vocabulary

drama takes over the whole session. Chapter 2 explains that drama can take place within many different time-frames and group sizes. It might be a five-minute starter stimulus or a 15-minute presentation of work at the end of a lesson. It may involve three pairs in role-play with a teaching assistant or it may include the whole class responding to you in character. In other words, drama can be used at any appropriate time during literacy sessions to support and enhance the teaching, whilst maintaining the focus on learning objectives for writing. Some examples of relevant activities are provided here and also in Chapter 10.

The writer in role

When children write in role, they can benefit in various ways. Let us consider these by looking at the example of a child filling in a booking form for a holiday. They are in role as a travel agent. Benefits to working in this way include:

- *providing the writing task with a sense of purpose* i.e. the form will be for a customer who is also in role
- *developing an understanding of when and why to use particular skills* e.g. fills in the form legibly because it is an important document
- *using reference skills as part of the role* e.g. checks the spelling of a town in the brochure
- *linking reading and writing* e.g. checking what has been written
- *making links between speaking and writing* e.g. answering questions that are then written on the form
- *using real texts as models* e.g. finding files, booking forms and information from brochures
- *providing an audience for the writing* e.g. the customer for checking or a 'clerk' at head office who then issues the tickets.

Children are usually very highly motivated when working in this way because it is fun, it is non-threatening, it is pretending to be a grown-up (which children of all ages usually love to do!) and it has a 'real' purpose. Such an atmosphere for learning is productive and effective, provided that the intended learning outcomes are carefully planned and monitored.

Another important feature of the 'writer in role' model is that it helps the child develop an empathy with the writer in ways that are particularly useful for certain genres. The examples that follow show extracts of children's writing that have been written in role. These were in response to an experience that also took place in role. Figure 6.1 is a poem by Laura (Year 1) which has been written after an exploration of how animals in zoos might feel about people staring at them all day. Laura wrote the poem in the role of a kangaroo. Figure 6.2 is an extract from a memo written by Daisy (Year 5) in role as a health inspector during a wider topic on healthy lifestyles. Each of these pieces was written after preparatory improvisational work (each taking 10 minutes including discussion), designed specifically for the purpose of creating stimuli and empathy for the writing.

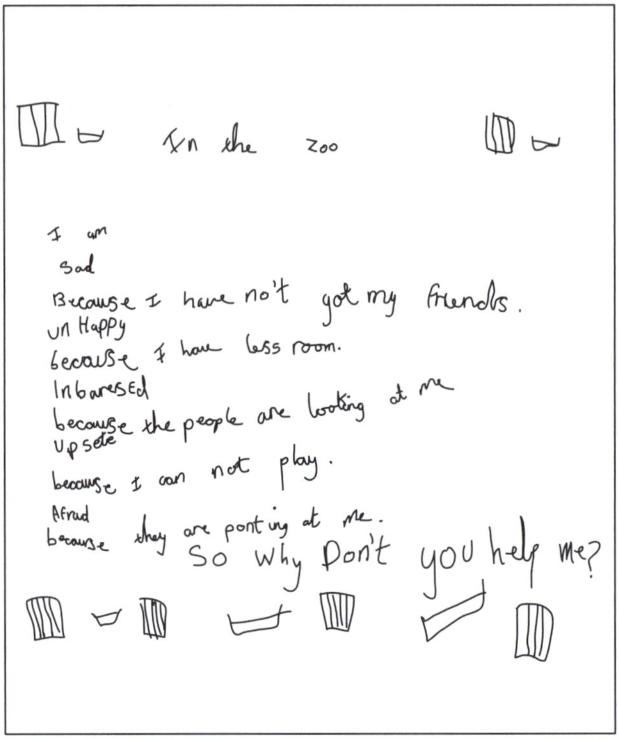

In the zoo

I am
Sad
Because I have no't got my friends.
un Happy
because I have less room.
Inbaresed
because the people are looking at me
Upsete
because I can not play.
Afrad
because they are ponting at me.
So why Don't you help me?

FIGURE 6.1 Written by Laura in the role of a kangaroo.

No matter how imaginative we believe children to be, they will always produce writing of a higher quality if we provide good stimuli for writing. If we expect children to write we need to give them something worthwhile to write about, and improvisations such as these provide starting points from which ideas can grow and develop, and with which the imagination can play.

Audience awareness

The other side of the writing coin is, of course, the reader or audience of the text. The drama can provide an audience for the writing in addition to, or instead of, providing an audience for the drama itself. If children are going to learn how to meet the needs of different audiences by writing in a range of ways they need to understand the intended readers' perspectives. This is what is known as 'accommodating the audience' (Frank, 1992: *passim*), and can be done in three main ways.

1. *Teacher in role.* If you are in role, requiring writing from the children for a purpose relating to that role, their thought processes will be extended into a more analytical mode of cognition. In other words, the writing process will actively involve the children in taking your needs as a reader into consideration. For example, you are in role as the hen in *Rosie's Walk* (Hutchins, 1970). You tell the children about what a wonderful walk you've just had, totally unaware of

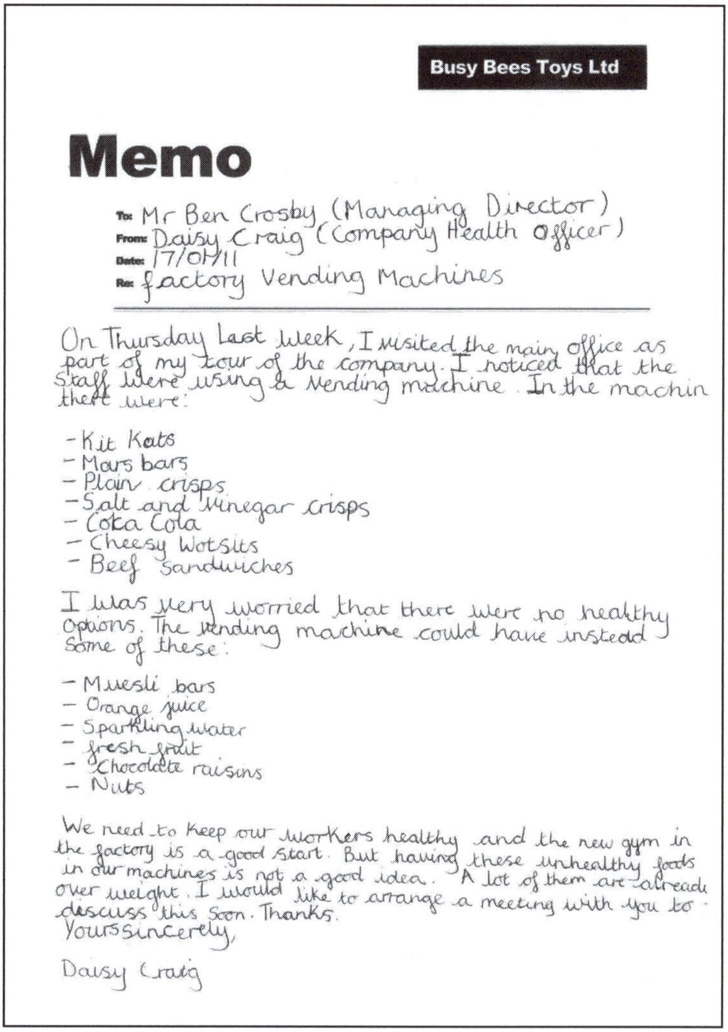

Busy Bees Toys Ltd

Memo

To: Mr Ben Crosby (Managing Director)
From: Daisy Craig (Company Health Officer)
Date: 17/01/11
Re: Factory Vending Machines

On Thursday last week, I visited the main office as part of my tour of the company. I noticed that the staff were using a vending machine. In the machine there were:

- Kit Kats
- Mars bars
- Plain crisps
- Salt and vinegar crisps
- Coca Cola
- Cheesy Wotsits
- Beef Sandwiches

I was very worried that there were no healthy options. The vending machine could have instead some of these:

- Muesli bars
- Orange juice
- Sparkling water
- Fresh fruit
- Chocolate raisins
- Nuts

We need to keep our workers healthy and the new gym in the factory is a good start. But having these unhealthy foods in our machines is not a good idea. A lot of them are already over weight. I would like to arrange a meeting with you to discuss this soon. Thanks.

Yours sincerely,

Daisy Craig

FIGURE 6.2 Written by Daisy in the role of a health officer.

the dangers of the fox. They may try to warn you about the fox, but you don't believe them. Out of role, you then discuss how they might help Rosie, by writing to her. What would be the best thing to write? A letter? Warning posters around the farm? Notes pinned to fences? Provide paper of different sizes and a range of writing materials for them to do their writing. Set a time limit. 'Rosie will be back in ten minutes! See how well you can write your warnings, and we'll give them to her when she returns.' (Or you might pin them around the room for Rosie to read as she enacts her farmyard stroll.) She will, of course, respond to the posters or letters! Reading these with the children is linking the writing and reading explicitly so that children are also learning to make the links for themselves. This example almost always results in the children then wanting to write to the fox!

2. *Reading in role.* The children read texts in role and discuss their responses. They then write for the reader whose role they have just taken. For example, in role as sorters at the post office, they have to decipher some badly written envelopes (which you provide). The envelopes are confusing because the handwriting is poor and the punctuation is used incorrectly. Ask them to decode the envelopes and make new labels in their best handwriting to stick over the top so the post-man will know where to deliver the letters.

3. *Interactional roles.* This is where children are playing roles in which they have to write for each other or to each other. For example, in role as two characters from a story, letter writing could become an ongoing activity. Providing a post box and pigeon holes or in-trays for delivery adds to the excitement of this.

4. *Reader research.* In this approach, the children carry out research in role, then write in a different role or out of role. For example, in pairs they role-play market research interviews between magazine writers and teenagers about the sorts of things that teenagers like to know about pop stars. The writers make notes. After three minutes, they change roles and change partners, so that everyone ends up with a set of notes. Finally, in a third and different partnership, the two look at the notes and write an article (out of role) about an imaginary pop star using the ideas given by the potential 'readers' of the magazine. As always, it is important to enrich the learning with visual aids and real examples. Remember that not all children are exposed to a range of texts at home. Handling the real thing, whether it is a letter, newspaper or baked bean tin, promotes interest and better learning. In this case, examples of magazines should be available to examine and discuss, to help the children develop an understanding of style, content and presentation.

Editing in role

Editing written material can sometimes seem a tedious task, especially for younger children. Indeed, it is not always necessary to write more than one draft; it depends on the purpose and genre of the writing. However, when writing does need to be put through several improvement processes (plan – first draft – edit – second draft – seek response – final draft – proofread – publish) it can help to create roles that will help the children to see the purpose of the process and also to make it more interesting. Examples of this might include:

■ transferring a doctor's notes onto a report card (role-play area)
■ exchanging work and 'marking' in role as the teacher
■ birthday card designers planning in teams
■ newspaper teams with editorial control
■ practising handwriting in a Victorian classroom.

Position of the drama

There is no single formula for how the drama relates to the writing. A useful way of considering the variety of options open to you is to think about the position of the drama in relation to the writing. There are three identifiable places where the drama might fit.

1. Writing before the drama

    Writing as a stimulus in preparation for drama; for example the children are asked to write letters which bring some good news. The letters are then placed in a box and shuffled. The children are organised into groups of four representing a family having breakfast. One member of the family goes to collect a letter (randomly chosen from the box) and the children improvise their response to the letter.

2. Writing during the drama

    The writing takes place in role during the drama, either as a spontaneous response to the action, or as an event that you have planned into the activity. One obvious place for this to happen is in a role-play area, as children write appointments, messages, lists, notes and so on as part of their play. However, the quality of this will depend very much on the provision. A home area that has telephone directories, memo pads, headed notepaper, envelopes, address books, greetings cards and so on will promote far more developmental writing activities than the home area that does not. Remember also that even Year 6 cool dudes enjoy role-play areas!

3. Writing after the drama

    Drama can provide a powerful stimulus for writing as explained earlier in this chapter. The quality of children's writing is influenced by the quality of the input beforehand. Opportunities for exploring, using and hearing varied vocabulary in discussion, and experiencing events from alternative perspectives can all contribute to the writing by boosting children's ideas, confidence and understanding of what they are to write about. For example: a meeting between local councillors and young people who are campaigning for a skateboard park will generate many more ideas and emotions than simply a prolonged class discussion while sitting on the carpet.

Examples of positioning are provided in the next section (see Table 6.2) in relation to the exemplification of range and genres.

Fiction, non-fiction and poetry

The range of texts that children should encounter in connection with reading and writing can be covered well in drama. The variables already discussed, in particular the timing of the drama, can be applied flexibly with all genres. Story writing can develop out of prior drama activities (role-play, improvisation, simulation, dynamic duos etc.), and indeed the drama can really help the ideas to flow, grow and develop!

Similarly, non-fiction texts (particular 'real world texts' such as documents, forms and leaflets) can have a relevant place within drama. If real texts are there during the experience, they are also providing models of writing for the children to emulate. Table 6.2 provides some examples of how writing can be located in three different positions with drama for different types of texts.

Providing responses to children's writing

Children need and enjoy constructive responses to their work. It motivates them, it teaches them and it completes the cycle of communication. Responses can come from a variety of sources: peers, other classes, other teachers, family, relatives, local

TABLE 6.2 Examples of drama for different genres

TYPE OF TEXT	WRITING BEFORE DRAMA	WRITING DURING DRAMA	WRITING AFTER DRAMA
Historical story	Writing a narrative to accompany a mime	Not appropriate	Improvisation or guided simulation to generate ideas for the story
Fairy tale	Writing a story for another group to enact	Not appropriate to write, but stories could be read during the drama	Beginning, middle and end tableaux to create basic structure of the story prior to writing
Report	Writing a report to 'broadcast'	Role-play writing as journalists in a simulated situation	Write report in role after a simulation or performance
List	Write a list prior to role-playing a visit to the shops	Write list of ideas from others – all in role	Write a list of events that took place during the drama
Instructions	Write a set of instructions for something that will then be randomly selected by another pair to act out	Role-play the writing of instructions for an explorer or treasure hunter	Write instructions for another group to recreate the drama that has just been devised
Biography	Research and write a biography that will then be used to answer questions in a hot seat	Take notes while interviewing a famous star in order to write their biography	Write a biography after watching a performed interview by other children
Play script	Plan and write a script to perform	Not appropriate	Write a script after an improvisation in order to structure ideas into a repeatable form
Poetry	Create soundbites to accompany freeze-frame sequence	Not appropriate	Write poetry in response to ideas generated during drama or after watching others perform

businesses, media, visitors and even famous people in some cases. Of course you are the central person whose response perhaps children depend upon more than anyone else's, and you are also responsible for coordinating the range of potential responses from others.

Planning writing activities so that responses are built into the process can make a tremendously enriching contribution to children's learning. Here are two examples:

 KS1 *EXAMPLE* **Messages to the imp**

A naughty imp is hiding somewhere in your classroom. Every night he comes out and makes a mess (which you all find each morning). So far he has tipped paintbrushes onto the carpet, ripped some newspapers all over the floor, and emptied out the multi-link. (Avoid paint and glue for this experience!) The children are encouraged to write messages to him about this situation. Needless to say, he writes messages back! How will the imp respond?

KS2 *EXAMPLE* **Publishing stories**

If the children are making books for the school library, this might be done with you in role as editor, and with them in role as real authors, formalising the process, and resulting in an interchange of comments, emails, phone messages and so on!

Useful resources for drama and writing

Resources in schools do not always have to depend on funding. There are many items that can be obtained free and which will help to support children's learning about writing. For instance, texts such as:

- information leaflets
- bus timetables
- newspapers
- magazines
- comics
- food packaging
- posters
- junk mail
- flyers
- tickets

- receipts
- telephone directories.

These can be used in drama to model writing structures, and to use in children's play and role-play.

Computer-generated resources

Desktop publishing software offers a rich array of ready-made formats for writing. Even if you reproduce these to be completed by hand for planning, they can offer plausible frameworks for children's writing which feel important and valid, for example a police report form, a business memo, a menu, a school report, an application form, a payment slip, an order form.

Enhancing writing areas through drama

Setting up writing areas in classrooms, particularly in the early years and KS1, is a recognised part of good practice. This is likely to include a good selection of different types, shapes and colours of paper; different writing tools; booths where children can work independently; examples of professional writing; dictionaries; word walls; and so on. Developing this one stage further so there are opportunities for role-play, for example turning it into an 'office', can further enhance the area, providing further encouragement for children to write on their own. To promote the interest of boys in particular, changing this according to their interests will provide the extra motivation needed: for example a garage office, a building supplier's desk or a football manager's office. Equipment in this area might include:

- forms
- receipt books
- catalogues
- phone
- message pad
- calendar
- diary
- whiteboard and pens
- dictionaries
- phone directories
- computer with email
- e-mail simulation (if you don't yet have the real thing)
- message book
- appointment book
- post box
- a pigeon hole or in-tray for each child.

Every school has parents and carers who work in offices, banks or other businesses that may be willing to provide office stationery and texts to add to the authenticity of the classroom office. Often, companies discard large quantities of stationery when they change their logo or brand image.

With thoughtful planning and relatively inexpensive resources it is possible to provide meaningful contexts for children's writing that will lead to:

- increased engagement and motivation
- higher levels of enjoyment
- better productivity
- higher attainment.

Providing reasons for reading

The complexity of reading

The reason we read is to access meaning for an infinite number of purposes. The enjoyment and appreciation of literature is one example of why we might read, but we also read in other ways and for other practical purposes: a shopping list as a reminder; a poster to find out details of an event; a contract to check what we are signing; directions to find our way to a venue. This requires us to:

- locate and select appropriate texts
- interact with texts
- respond to texts.

These processes are intellectually dynamic and interrogatory – it is not necessarily easy to learn how to select, use and respond to texts without meaningful purpose and

relevant contexts. Drama is an ideal way of providing children with a multitude of reasons for reading. Creating different authentic 'reading situations' through the drama
means they can interact with texts and in doing so become proactive and responsive
readers. This chapter helps you to understand how you might plan for this to happen
in your classroom, but first let us take a closer look at other relevant aspects of the
teaching of reading.

Reading is a complex process involving different strategies that operate together at
different levels to create meaning from text. To read a text we need to be able to:

- recognise the shapes of the letters and words (graphemic knowledge)
- relate these to the sounds they make (phonemic knowledge)
- interpret the ways in which the words are organised to make meaning from the
  grammar (syntactic knowledge)
- interpret the words and context into meaning (semantic knowledge).

Although there may appear to be a hierarchical progression to these four strategies, in reality they operate simultaneously. However, children who are just starting
to read need to direct more of their effort into decoding skills, which is why it is so
important to provide early readers with books at the right level of difficulty. Research
shows that children who are struggling with a text that is far beyond their grapho-
phonemic knowledge are so busy focusing on the letters and sounds that they are not
accessing meaning (Clay, 1979; Stanovich, 1980). This is usually why, when we listen
to children reading in this laborious way, they are unable to answer questions about
the story very accurately when they reach the end. As they develop into more fluent
readers, the first two strategies become more automatic, and the proportion of time
spent attending to meaning and responding increases.

It is also important to remember that decoding and understanding texts is only part
of the process. The *raison d'être* of reading is response. Responding to texts can mean
many different things, from reading that shopping list to engaging in a fierce debate
about the sentimentality (or not!) of Heathcliff in *Wuthering Heights*. All too often in
schools, the focus is too heavily on the decoding, at worst in de-contextualised texts
that do nothing to engage children in the pleasure and purpose of reading. Children
need to understand right from the start that they are learning to read because it is a
tool that they will use all of their lives for a vast multitude of purposes. If children are
going to develop this understanding of how different modes of response are required
by different text situations they will need to interact with texts in ways that will elicit
a range of responses.

There have been concerns in recent years that children are losing interest in books
and that reading standards are declining. There are many reasons for this, but the
solutions offered are too few and too narrow. Governments continue to focus on the
place of phonics as the definitive answer, and there is no doubt that these building
blocks of reading are vital. However, the teaching of reading should be taught within
a rich literacy environment where texts are valued, enjoyed and seen to be useful by
children. Drama can make a valuable contribution to this for readers of all ages in the
primary school by offering models of reading, and contexts for reading that help them

to perceive themselves as readers in the real world. A new model to illustrate this was developed from *Reading On! Developing Reading at Key Stage 2* (Clipson-Boyles, 1996). The description and diagram of the new model are reproduced in the next section (see Figure 7.1).

A model of interaction between drama and reading

The National Curriculum for English requires children to respond and relate to a wide variety of texts. To do this, they need to read for a range of purposes, and employ different reading skills at different times. They are required to develop a knowledge of literature and the confidence to express their own views about what they have read. To do this, they need to be efficient and selective in the retrieval of information from different sources. Such requirements demand interactive models of learning, and drama is an ideal way of providing activities to extend and develop pupils as responsive readers.

The simple model presented here demonstrates the potential relationship between drama and reading to provide engagement, enjoyment and meaningful reasons to read. There are arguably five key components of reading: graphemic/phonemic (to decode the text), syntactic (to construct grammatical order from the decoded text), semantic (to construct meaning), comprehension (to understand and interpret that meaning) and response (to react to or act upon what has been understood). These components of reading become increasingly interwoven although they do not necessarily develop at the same time or pace. Decoding is more dominant in the early stages of learning to read, though response is nevertheless a vital part of enjoying reading, stories in particular. More advanced readers decode automatically, moving almost

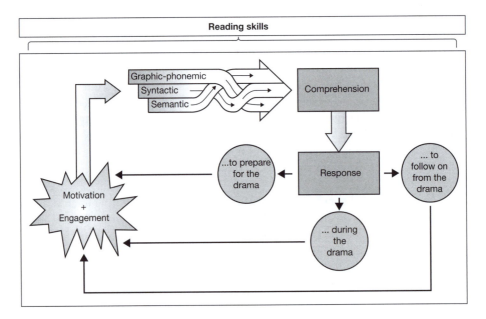

FIGURE 7.1 A new model of interaction between drama and reading.

simultaneously with response. The development of the reader into an increasingly sophisticated interrogator of texts takes place from birth through to adulthood. At KS2, graphemic/phonemic awareness and syntactic competence are, for the majority of pupils, well established, although semantic skills may vary for different ability levels. The responsive capabilities of older readers will now be ripe for a more rapid rate of growth as the need to focus on the basics of reading will reduce. Figure 7.1 illustrates how drama can act as a catalyst for reading by providing reasons to read before, during or after the drama.

The model illustrates how the drama can mobilise the reading activity in one of three ways, and in doing so helps to motivate and engage the children by providing a meaningful context. In other words, the drama can provide a vehicle for the reading and vice versa. Let us look more closely at each part of the model.

Application and practice of reading skills

Children will not develop as readers unless they read, but in KS2 there is a considerable shift towards independent reading and this can sometimes mean that the reader is left to cope alone without the necessary skills to get the best out of the activity. The reading might take place without any increase in the level of response. The model illustrates how the drama can provide a reason for the reading to take place that will engage the children. This experience, in turn, will provide opportunities to learn and practise the key components mentioned earlier. Comprehension will be vital to the use of the reading task.

The pupil response

Pupil response is the least likely component of reading to develop directly from independent reading activities. Drama addresses the interactive nature of response by facilitating discussion, exploration, action and debate. The reader response box in the model represents the *raison d'être* for reading, and yet there are usually too few opportunities in primary schools for this to happen. The response component is the most appropriate aspect of reading to be developed through drama and might include any number of different types of response, for example an action, an interpretation, an emotion, an analysis or a disagreement.

Pupil motivation

The lack of motivation to read is of growing concern to teachers and indeed the wider world. This can result in a lack of enthusiasm for fiction, poor knowledge of authors, reluctance to try something new, or lack of engagement with books as a source of information. To overcome such potential deficits in this vital aspect of literacy, teachers need to ensure that children are motivated to read.

The position of the drama activity

Drama is usually enjoyed by most children; lessons are characterised by enthusiasm, energy and commitment. Such positive attitudes to learning can be harnessed to deliver an exciting and productive approach to reading development. The reading can be situated in one of three places in relation to the drama (as for writing, explained in Chapter 6). Here are some examples to illustrate this.

- *Before the drama:* reading a newspaper article to extract information and develop a three-part tableaux presentation
- *During the drama:* a character reads out a letter to which other characters respond in an improvisation
- *After the drama:* research on the Internet to answer their own questions generated during a simulation of the Great Fire of London.

However, although motivation and engagement have a huge impact on the quality of learning, they do not necessarily guarantee that children will make enough progress. It is therefore important to be very clear and precise about what different ability groups might be learning as a result of the activity. This is discussed in more detail in Chapter 10.

The value that drama can add to reading

You will, by now, be familiar with the principles of experiential learning through drama and the range of approaches that are available to you. You will also recognise that drama can embrace such learning in harmony with language work, cross-curricular language skills and theatre arts, each integrating with the other or not, according to the aims of the activity. All these elements offer contexts for reading activities. Here are some examples.

Props that will be used in role-play

Newspapers, telephone directories and recipe books in the role-play area will be used by children in play and extend their concepts of print and awareness of purposes for reading. Older children can be given texts to read during improvisation, such as a letter to stimulate response, a newspaper article to provide information for a police interview and so on.

Exploring storyline

Re-enactment of stories in their own language can provide an enjoyable reason for shared reading beforehand.

Exploring beyond the storyline

Additional parts of the story, alternative endings, expanding implicit parts of the story, can be played out during improvisation, and also worked into small-scale performance.

Understanding character motivation

Taking sections of story to explore why characters acted in certain ways, or improvising characters' thoughts, can lead to useful analysis, and train children into thinking more deeply about text and subtext.

Sequencing and performing story

Giving story sections to children and asking them to sequence the sections and to present their work to others is a good reading-for-meaning task. Exploring the effects of changing the sequence can provide opportunities for further analysis and discussion about story structure.

Researching for the drama

Use of information books can provide material for drama, for instance creating tableaux or plays about the Ancient Greeks, to share with the rest of the class. Further discussion about the parts which were fact and those which were fiction offers scope for justification and accountability by giving references in answer to questioning by the others after their presentation.

Research arising from the drama

Sometimes, themes or issues will emerge during the drama that will benefit from further research afterwards, particularly in combination with follow-up writing activities.

Word games

Charades which have to include new vocabulary can involve reading first in order to select those words.

Information needed for script writing

Script writing might be in response to prior improvisation that has prompted further research, or may require reading in order to search for ideas.

Preparation for simulation

Sometimes, a simulation can be planned and prepared by the children rather than by you. This will require research, for example: How is a newsroom set out? Who works there? What will be on their desks? What sort of equipment do you find in offices?

Starting points for presentations

Presentation might mean puppet show, radio interview, tableaux sequence etc. The reading can be a starting point for this, e.g. a story reported in a newspaper, a letter.

Models for writing in role

The National Curriculum states repeatedly that children should be shown models of good practice in writing. If we expect children to produce a poster, they need to see lots of different examples of posters and discuss the features. Writing in role is also enhanced by the provision of 'real' texts because it helps the children to pretend.

You may have noticed, as you read these examples, that, as explained for writing in the previous chapter, the reading can connect with the drama at different times:

- *before the drama:* e.g. as preparation or stimulus
- *during the drama:* e.g. as prop for role-play, for reading aloud, as instruction
- *after the drama:* e.g. follow-up inquiry, reading responses, further information.

These alternative positions will affect the reading interrogation strategies, because the purpose will be different each time. This is a good argument for varying the positioning of the reading when planning drama activities.

Another important area for consideration has to be the range of texts that you provide for these activities. How can you provide an exciting range of texts, and how do you go about equipping your classroom with such vast quantities of reading materials? How do you contextualise the activities for the children, and why is it so necessary to go to all this trouble? Let us look at this more closely.

Using different types of texts in drama

If children are going to develop a response repertoire and become proactive independent readers they need to understand that in our society there is a vast range of things to read. This principle is endorsed by the National Curriculum requirements. Children should be provided with opportunities to speak and write for a range of purposes, in a range of styles and for a range of audiences. Likewise, with reading, teachers are expected to provide children with a range of genres, and of texts within those genres. The National Curriculum expects a comprehensive and systematic approach to teaching reading and writing at word, sentence and text levels, and offers guidance on text range by recommending different genres of fiction, poetry and non-fiction for each term of primary schooling. This not only ensures that there is good coverage of genres for every child but also helps teachers to plan activities which combine the systematic teaching of strategies within a range of literary contexts. Children need to use and develop reading and writing through meaningful activities that relate to 'real' texts rather than practising language exercises in a dissociated vacuum. Drama is an invaluable teaching approach with which you can help children to learn effectively in this way.

Providing a variety of texts enables children to adopt different approaches to reading according to the type of text and the purpose. Texts other than fiction demand a wide range of reading interrogation strategies, sometimes even within the same booklet or magazine. For example a football programme might be read by comparing the players on each team before a match. This would involve scanning, focusing in, cross-referencing from one to another to compare, and responding by assessing the chances of each team based on the selection. On the other hand, in another section of the same programme, a feature article on the captain would require reading through from beginning to end.

Encountering different categories of texts helps to:

- broaden children's concepts of textual diversity
- expand their perceptions of themselves as readers
- increase their repertoire of reading interrogation strategies
- stimulate their interest in reading.

It can be helpful to group texts into categories when planning to use drama to help children interact with and respond to texts. A model of six categories is presented in Table 7.1 with some examples of how the drama might link into each category. This is not a definitive categorisation, and there are obvious areas of overlap where certain texts might fit into more than one category, but the model is a useful way to identify potential texts, and use their associated sources as a starting point for drama (e.g. contracts = employment scenario).

Reading interrogation strategies

Having discussed the range of purposes and the variety of texts that children need to encounter, let us now think about the range of strategies that they might use to extract information when reading.

Here are some examples of different reading interrogation strategies (RIS) being used during drama. The six text categories are represented, one in each example.

YEAR 1 EXAMPLE   **Justifying decisions**

TEXT: *Would You Rather . . .* (Burningham, 1994)

CATEGORY: Literature

ACTIVITY: Improvisations of some of the activities in the book, then choosing from the alternatives offered ('Would you rather have . . . supper in a castle, breakfast in a balloon, or tea on the river?')

RIS: Reading for meaning, comparing, decision making, justifying decisions

---

TABLE 7.1 Categories of text with drama examples

	LITERATURE	NON-FICTION	REFERENCE	LEISURE TEXTS	COMMERCIAL TEXTS	DOCUMENTS
Example	Children's own writing Novels Picture books Plays Poetry Short stories	Biographies Coffee-table books Hobbies/interests Manuals Recipes/DIY Textbooks	Atlases Databases Dictionaries Directories Encyclopaedias Internet Timetables	Cartoon books Comics Joke books Magazines Newspapers Football programmes TV guides	Advertisements Catalogues Flyers Labels Leaflets Posters Price lists	Contracts Faxes Forms Letters Memos Minutes Reports
Some functions of the drama	Explore character Develop storyline Perform Sequencing	Use for research Use in role-play Explore beyond a picture Answer questions after drama	Reference in role-play Word games Seek information for script writing Information for simulation	Props for characters Character information Story starting points Making news programmes	Business role-play Props and scenery Starting point for improvisation Models for writing in role	Office role-play Writing in role Artefacts as stimulus for improvisation Follow-up writing

YEAR 2 EXAMPLE   **Radio programme on karate**

TEXT: Selection of information books about karate

CATEGORY: Non-fiction/leisure texts/commercial texts

ACTIVITY: Research from texts to write and present a radio programme, 'Karate through the Keyhole: A 5-Minute Tour!' (Other hobbies could also be used.)

RIS: Reading for information, comparing, selecting, sequencing and communicating the information in a new form

YEAR 3 EXAMPLE   **Fixing the washing machine**

TEXT: Yellow Pages/report forms/instruction leaflets

CATEGORY: Reference

ACTIVITY: After explanation of Yellow Pages and washing machine instruction leaflet, provide overalls, tools, report forms. Role-play/practise/show

RIS: Alphabetical sequence/reading for information

YEAR 4 EXAMPLE   **Footballer interview**

TEXT: Football magazine

CATEGORY: Leisure texts

ACTIVITY: Give them a star interview to read and ask them to establish what sorts of things are asked. Improvise interviews, trying to remember the information, OR with 'new' stars, inventing different information which can then be written into a new article

RIS: Reading for information/analysis of sections

YEAR 5 EXAMPLE　　　　　**Cafe role-play**

TEXT: Selection of menus

CATEGORY: Commercial texts

ACTIVITY: Show and discuss menus. Groups of four pretend to be new cafe owners planning the opening of a new cafe. Design posters and menus (in role)

RIS: Reading for information/seeking spellings/learning format

YEAR 6 EXAMPLE　　　　**Redesigning parkland**

TEXT: Report (created by you) about the proposed redesign of the local park

CATEGORY: Documents

ACTIVITY: Put children in role as local community action group. In role as councillor, give each group a copy of the report to discuss. Ask for list of responses, to be presented to council meeting

RIS: Reading for information/analysis of separate points/responding to each point

Reading and exploring play scripts

We have been looking, so far, at how drama can serve the reading process. It is also worth considering how literature can actually feed into the drama, in particular play scripts. Reading plays is a requirement of the National Curriculum. Children love reading plays and reading plays in groups is particularly beneficial to young children's reading development because:

- the group situation is social and enjoyable
- reading together provides inbuilt support
- the turn-taking breaks the reading into bite-size chunks
- the children are encouraged to read ahead so they are ready for their next turn
- children rarely wander off-task because they have to be ready to read at different points
- the implicit purpose is to create meaning
- interpreting stage directions (when they are included) offers a good context for reading for meaning and following instruction
- dramatising the play gives additional support to accessing the meaning

- dramatising the play encourages reading with expression
- dramatising the play encourages fluent reading
- rereading and rehearsing for a purpose (i.e. performance) offers children a non-threatening reason to aim for a higher standard without feeling they are failing.

Plays were written to be performed, but there are many playwrights, the Bard included, who would be horrified if they could see the tortured ways in which pupils in some secondary schools are asked to dissect and interpret their texts without even so much as five minutes of action during the hour's lesson! In recent years, this secondary approach to teaching English has leaked into some primary classrooms, and it has not helped to promote better learning. Drama is essential when learning about plays, and it is also a valuable way of exploring other types of literature. Let us look at some of the scripts that you might explore with your children.

Reading-scheme plays

Many commercial reading schemes include play scripts: for example Oxford Reading Tree (OUP); Fuzzbuzz Plays (OUP); New Reader Plays (Longman Book Project); Primary Whodunnit Plays (Collins); and the Active Drama Play Scripts series (Evans Brothers Ltd). This is a useful way of resourcing script reading activities because they are usually sold in multi-copy packs for groups. Some even come in extra-large packs to equip a full class.

Plays for older children

In addition to reading-scheme books, older readers enjoy working with scripts from plays that have been written for the theatre. In addition to the benefits in the previous list, this approach adds further value because:

- it helps to broaden their knowledge of literature
- it introduces them to famous playwrights
- they can start to make links with real theatre
- they can compare styles of writing
- they can look at plays historically
- there are more detailed stage directions demanding more complex interpretation.

Most large public libraries have drama sections from which you can borrow sets of play scripts for extended periods. It is advisable to read through the plays yourself first if you don't know them. Plays offer a range of genres: thrillers, musicals, classics, historical, pantomime, children's plays and so on. It is unlikely that you would ever wish children to read a play in its entirety, although the option to read on independently is an excellent way of extending more able readers.

Remember also that some extracts can offer a self-contained story within a scene. You may wish to use an extract as a stimulus for improvising and then writing an alternative ending or beginning. A good example of this is the dramatic final scene in

Brecht's *Caucasian Chalk Circle* (2007). Grusha and Natella have come to court so that the judge, Azdak, can decide which young woman is the real mother of the child. He resolves the conflict, in his wisdom, by drawing a chalk circle and placing the child in the centre. He instructs the two women to each take one of the child's arms and pull. Whoever pulls the child out of the circle is to keep him. Each time, Grusha lets go of the child's arm for fear of hurting him, and Azdak knows that she is indeed the true mother. This scene is critically tense, and children enjoy building up the dramatic moments. Working out their own stories about how this situation emerged can result in some wonderful written work and further drama! Avid readers nearly always want to read the missing parts of the play afterwards!

The place of Shakespeare in the primary school

A significant number of secondary school pupils struggle with Shakespeare. (Many adults also struggle with Shakespeare! You might be one of them . . . If you are, read on!) It is a sad reality that Shakespeare's plays are regarded by many as irrelevant or even unattainable for them. An academic and somewhat elitist barrier exists that prevents many people from believing that these plays have any part to play in their lives. This is possibly due to the endless analysis, dissection, debate, controversy and intellectual possession that has taken over ownership of these plays. Shakespeare himself would not be happy with this state of affairs! His plays were written to be performed and enjoyed by all people. In his time they were acted out in the streets of towns and village squares to all and sundry, and they were extremely popular.

If children encounter some of Shakespeare's stories in primary school, they are more likely to approach their studies later with confidence and a better understanding. Perhaps more importantly, they will feel 'ownership' of this part of our heritage and be more motivated to visit theatres to see his plays of their own accord later in life.

Shakespeare in the primary school should be approached initially through story. The stories are wonderful, and children will enjoy hearing you tell them, either in your own words or from one of the many splendid abridged versions that are available for younger children. Shakespeare can also be set in the context of a wider cross-curricular topic, for example the Tudors. Here are some examples of cross-curricular activities around *Macbeth* that could be planned as part of your wider work on Shakespeare:

- creating atmosphere: telling a spooky story of three witches in a darkened room using a torch
- puppet performance to play out parts of the story
- improvise short sections to explore themes
- making thematic mobiles (e.g. daggers, crowns, cauldrons)
- abstract art work of themes and moods (fear, pride, haunted heath)
- making model play sets (castles)
- shortened versions of the play for assembly
- playing with parts of language – experimenting with some of the stranger words

- writing and drawing cartoon strips of scenes
- creating backing sound effects (e.g. to represent a roaring wind or bubbling cauldron)
- discussion from clips of video or animated versions.

'Doing Shakespeare' does not mean taking on a whole play in its original entirety. Focusing on short sections can often be more productive with primary children, and certainly offers enough scope for activities (e.g. the Pyramus and Thisbe play within *A Midsummer Night's Dream*).

All these suggestions have been successfully tried and tested with eight- to eleven-year-olds! Their enthusiasm was immense, and the real thrill for me as a teacher was to meet one of them six years later and hear him say, 'I'm the best at Shakespeare in my set! I loved it when we did *The Dream* in your class!' (He was one of the boys seen chasing round the playground when he was eight yelling 'Away, ye vile canker blossoms'!)

Making the most of free resources

Good-quality resources are crucial to good-quality teaching, but we all know that high costs can be involved in the purchase of books. However, there is a wealth of free reading material out there that can also be obtained for use in the classroom. As well as the cost savings, there are additional advantages:

- You can collect sets (e.g. six catalogues, 15 theme park leaflets, 30 pizza menus).
- You can involve business and commercial partners in education (e.g. local shops, tourist information, restaurants).
- You can involve parents and carers and help them to understand the breadth of the reading repertoire for their child (i.e. 'the reading book' is not the only thing to be read).
- Children enjoy the feeling of using 'real world' texts and pretending to be adults.
- It provides variety, which is the spice of learning as well as of life!

In some shops you can help yourself to leaflets, flyers and brochures; in some you will have to ask. It is also worth remembering that used items can be useful and free, for example newspapers, TV guides, football programmes, theatre posters and comics. Most parents and carers, neighbours, friends and relatives are usually only too happy to save these for you – better to recycle things for a worthwhile cause than throw them away!

English as an additional language

Chapter overview

This chapter aims to provide a simple overview of the reasons why and ways in which drama can support the language development of children who speak English as an additional language (EAL). It discusses:

■ language diversity in Britain

■ drama, inclusion and community cohesion

■ language and learning

■ drama and language

■ identifying the learning needs of EAL children

■ the impact of group interaction

■ useful drama techniques for EAL.

Language diversity in Britain

Cultural diversity continues to flourish in Britain and an increasingly wide range of languages is spoken by children in our schools. Indeed, many children are multilingual rather than bilingual. This rich tapestry of linguistic patterning can strengthen the language curriculum because it enables all children to observe and explore language within the context of actual usage and relate this directly to different cultures and traditions. To learn, understand and think in more than one language is an asset to children, and should not be regarded as a barrier that has to be overcome. Likewise, the monolingual English-speaking peers of children who speak other languages can benefit enormously from this additional dimension to language learning in school.

However, there are important educational implications for those children who are learning English as an additional language (EAL learners), and the first of these is to recognise that diversity requires high levels of teacher knowledge. The problem with labels such as 'bilingual learners', 'English as a second language' (ESL) and 'mother tongue' is that they can imply diluted generalities about children that are not always accurate. This can sometimes result in stereotyping and, as a consequence, lead to inappropriate teaching approaches.

The social contexts of bilingualism are complex. For instance, the term might include third-generation children in stable well-established British families, children in recently arrived families whose parents or carers are planning to settle in Britain for temporary periods of work, or even families escaping from political unrest in their homeland. The status of English also varies enormously within groups. Some families may use two languages, including English, at home; some children may be the only speakers of English in their family, commencing from when they start school; some may have parents or carers who speak two languages including English but are new to English themselves; others may belong to families where everyone speaks their community language in the home and English outside the home. These represent only some examples of the numerous variations, so the teacher's task is to establish not only the actual languages spoken by the children in their class, but also the part the languages play in the lives of the children and the customs and practices that accompany them.

Communication styles vary not only in the words spoken but also in the ways they are spoken. The rise and fall of tone, speed, volume, the way in which discourse is constructed, listening postures and other body language are all potent forces behind cultural differences. Knowledge of these can help teachers to understand and respect the whole language of the child, so that styles of English usage for different purposes can be compared and explained appropriately, rather than being 'imposed' as a superior model. For example, it is important to understand simple naming practices, and ensure that children's names are pronounced correctly. Should the form of address be the last name or the first? Is the name on school records the religious name or the family name? Should any of the names be used by family only? When teaching English as an additional language, teachers should recognise the importance and status of the child's own language. Respectful consideration of such issues makes a significant difference to the child's sense of security and willingness to learn. It is also important for teachers to recognise that children's first language has an important role to play in learning across the curriculum (see NALDIC, 2009).

Drama, inclusion and community cohesion

Regardless of the cultural mix of a school, it is important for all children to learn about the diverse and interesting composition of our multi-cultural communities here in Britain. Helping children to develop knowledge and understanding about the rich variety of customs, foods, languages, stories and religions can make an important contribution towards building a harmonious and cohesive society in which differences are respected, diversity celebrated and commonality enjoyed.

Drama can provide an invaluable approach to multi-cultural education, and building cohesive communities within school and beyond. At the surface informational level, it can be used to impart knowledge through interaction. For example, a simulation approach could be used to enable children to 'experience' and compare festivals such as weddings from different religions. However, at a deeper level, drama is also an effective way to approach more difficult issues, particularly with older children. For example, Jackie Kay's poem 'Duncan Gets Expelled' (1994), which is about racist bullying, offers a powerful way to introduce this topic. Using tableaux or freeze frame to construct the story of the poem provides a good platform for discussion and places the issue into a safe space by de-personalising it through the drama.

Multi-cultural education does not merely provide a backdrop for children learning English as an additional language. It has a vital part to play in building an inclusive environment within school, and can contribute to children's developing understanding of community cohesion in other communities beyond school. Effective teaching and learning in this area will be underpinned by the principles that multi-cultural education should:

- be provided for all
- work towards a better understanding through quality information and experiences
- offer a celebration of diversity rather than homogenisation
- not be afraid to tackle difficult issues
- always aim for positive outcomes.

Drama has a role to play in all these things, by promoting knowledge through experience, fostering empathy through active engagement, and offering a safety net of distance when dealing with sensitive issues. However, providing vibrant and inclusive contexts for multi-culturalism is only one aspect of learning to speak English as an additional language. It is also necessary to understand how this connects to and influences other aspects of children's learning.

Language and learning

Language is inextricably linked to our academic and cognitive development because we use language to think. The development of conceptual understanding and the growth of knowledge in all areas of the curriculum depend on the frameworks of language needed to explain, describe, discuss and challenge them. We use language to construct meaning, to dismantle meaning, and to redesign meaning. We use it to recall, remember, hypothesise, predict and so on. Clearly, where English is the only instructional language for the curriculum, EAL learners are not only learning a new language but also trying to make sense of their other learning in that language rather than in their own.

Studies in the United States have shown that, where EAL learners and their majority language peers were taught together in two languages across the curriculum, the EAL learners made much better progress than those taught in an all-English programme (Collier, 1992). The main reason for this was the fact that the EAL pupils were able to use their first language in order to develop concepts and skills and, as they continued to do this alongside English, the two eventually became interchangeable.

It would be impractical to expect such bilingual teaching to take place in all schools, particularly in classes where there is more than one language spoken in addition to English. However, Collier acknowledges that important elements of her research, in particular multi-culturalism, collaborative and interactive learning, and high levels of intellectual challenge, can be transported into everyday classroom practice. The educational implications here are very different from policies imposed some years ago when it was thought best to exclude the home language from the educational process. It is now recognised that in fact the home language has a vital role to play in the child's learning, and that giving the language status, taking an active interest in it and allowing the child to use it alongside English will help the child's progress, not only in their language development but also in their academic progress and conceptual development across all subjects.

Drama and language

It is important to distinguish between basic interpersonal communicative skills and cognitive and academic language proficiency when planning for learning. Bilingual children should be learning language across the curriculum as well as learning about the curriculum through language. Drama can set the context for learning language and learning about language, and earlier chapters have explained how drama can be used within different subjects as a medium for learning. Drama promotes active involvement, and can accommodate the integration of reading, writing and oracy in relevant and realistic contexts. It helps children to make sense of language and meaning, and offers the option of repetition in fun ways that can eliminate the boredom factor from tasks requiring repeated revision and recap. It provides situations in which children are required to construct knowledge, while at the same time offering the flexibility to revise and reconstruct that same knowledge. All of this takes place through listening, experimenting, reworking, modelling and imitating.

Drama enables children to work together in groups and involves high levels of discussion that leads directly to the development of ideas and concepts relating to both formal and informal linguistic situations. It also enables EAL learners to use their first language alongside English. Drama can be used to assist learning in various areas of the curriculum and thus offers a whole range of learning opportunities that can be used effectively in multi-lingual classrooms.

Identifying the learning needs of EAL pupils

Having taken the time and care to find out about the language background of the child, as described in the first section of this chapter, it is necessary to ascertain the level of fluency in English. Education authorities have different ways of categorising EAL learners, and this is used primarily to link need to funding. A basic framework called the Stages of English Learning (Hester, 1990) still provides a useful continuum for teachers to consider when planning for the needs of the children in their class. The stages are detailed under four headings:

Stage 1:   new to English

Stage 2:   becoming familiar with English

Stage 3:   becoming confident as a user of English

Stage 4:   very fluent user of English in most social and learning contexts.

Identifying the current level of fluency enables the teacher to plan the types of learning experiences that will most help the child. It is also important to distinguish between the language needs of the child and the cognitive challenge required. Varying approaches to support will be required accordingly. These might include:

- class teacher working with a group of EAL learners pupils and a support teacher working with the rest of the class
- support teacher working with a group of EAL learners pupils and the class teacher working with the rest of the class
- work within a small target group to supplement curricular learning with additional language input
- one-to-one support within the classroom to link the language learning to curricular language
- withdrawal for specific language teaching.

All these considerations should be underpinned with a sound knowledge of language acquisition. In relation to drama, the key principles of language learning include:

- meaningful contexts for the language (e.g. role-play in a shop)
- listening to the patterns of language (e.g. watching others perform their work)
- active participation (e.g. group planning)
- use of supportive resources (e.g. puppets)
- imitation of appropriate modelling (e.g. group improvisation)
- repetition (e.g. rereading play scripts)
- use of the home language (e.g. bilingual theatre/translation)
- motivation and security (e.g. the fun of drama).

The impact of group interaction

Providing a supportive environment for learning is vital. Language cannot be learned in isolation. It is a dynamic process that requires interaction between people. It therefore makes good educational sense to allow children to work collaboratively in groups where they can speak in a range of ways and learn to listen to one another. However, successful group management is a real challenge for the teacher if the children are to stay on task and engage with each other in ways which will help them to learn.

Groupings for drama will vary in size as already described in Chapter 3. When considering the needs of EAL learners there will also be the issue of levels of fluency and understanding to consider. Groupings will change according to the purpose of the activity and the particular learning needs of the individual. Here are some examples.

1. *Grouped with speakers of the same language:* to discuss and role-play ideas in the home language. Perform to others in home language with an English narration provided by a KS2 pupil.
2. *Grouped with monolingual English speakers:* to discuss and role-play ideas in English, with the possibility to translate into home language for others to hear.
3. *Mixed fluency plus English-speaking group:* to enable more fluent bilingual children to translate and interpret.

There is sometimes a risk that EAL children are not sufficiently challenged cognitively because of the prime focus on their language. One of the ways of ensuring that children's academic potential is maximised is to provide secure contexts for learning within groups of similar ability.

Useful drama techniques for EAL

Drama and story

Arguably, story is at the heart of all language learning. Stories have been told since history began, passed down through the ages, between generations and across cultures, many written down to be read. Every day, people can be heard telling real-life stories of things which have happened to them or others, and stories, real and imagined, are encapsulated in songs and poems and on television and cinema screens.

Stories transmit ideas, customs and traditions, but they also transmit language: meaning, vocabulary, sounds of rhythm and rhyme, sentence and narrative structure are all communicated through stories. So it is small wonder that telling and reading stories to children in school has long been considered to be an important part of primary education. Stories can also be used in other ways to teach language skills and drama has a useful part to play in offering a more active understanding in the following ways:

- miming the actions as the story is read
- miming the story as child retells in home language
- performing the story in English with child translator
- performing the story in home language with child translator
- puppet replay of the story
- improvising alternative endings to the story
- introducing new character into the story
- watching a professional performance of a story
- watching a film or TV performance of a story
- using cue cards with phrases from the story to make a new story.

These approaches should also be used with stories from a variety of cultures. Encouraging children to bring in stories from home not only expands your story supply but also gives encouraging messages to children about the status and value of their home language.

Working in role

There are different ways of working in role, as described in Chapter 2, and you should refer to these for more detailed descriptions of how you might use them. When working with EAL learners, role-play has four particular benefits that meet their language learning needs appropriately and effectively. These are:

1. the provision of 'real' contexts for the language

2. opportunities to hear others modelling the appropriate language

3. opportunities to practise language and take risks with new vocabulary and constructions in an enjoyable and non-threatening situation

4. opportunities to 're-run' or 'repeat' language scenarios in order to practise fluency and expression, and build confidence.

Reading plays

This activity clearly depends on the children's level of reading ability, but can be a good supporting bridge between dependent and independent reading. Plays can be read in different ways:

- in unison

- in pairs

- independently as characters.

Reading a play through several times gives the opportunity to practise fluency and expression, and adding movements and gestures not only makes it more fun but also entails discussion and explanation within the group, which is itself part of the learning process. Play scripts also offer opportunities for following instructions (stage directions).

Play scripts can also be written by the teacher in order to meet particular needs. These need not be long or time-consuming to produce, and can reap very immediate rewards in terms of language gains.

Provide a desk and writing materials to role-play the taking of details for a holiday booking. This provides an opportunity to practise asking and/or answering questions about personal details.

Travel agent:	What is your name?
Customer:	My name is . . . .
Travel agent:	What is your address?
Customer:	My address is . . . .
Travel agent:	What date would you like to travel?

Puppets

There are many different ways of making and using puppets, and these are described in Chapter 2. Puppets are an extremely useful resource to assist language learning for EAL pupils. Commercially produced puppets can be used to accompany the reading of books and listening to CDs and for spontaneous improvisation. An interesting and adaptable collection kept in the classroom is usually a tremendous stimulus for children, and a commercial or home-made puppet theatre can offer an appealing environment within which to explore and practise language. Some publishers sell puppets to accompany their reading schemes, and these can also provide additional access to meaning in the texts that children are reading.

Structuring the children's work around known stories, including those from different cultures, can also provide a scaffold on which they can build their own stories. Puppets that the children make themselves offer a further host of valuable learning experiences. First, the actual planning, designing and making of the puppets provides a context for using the language not only of the technology curriculum, but also of the story for which the puppets are intended. The story vocabulary assists the technology and the technology vocabulary assists the exploration of the story. For instance, descriptions of a character's appearance and behaviour, scene-setting for any background models, ways in which they will need to move in order to express their personality and so on can all be discussed during the course of this work.

Moving on to the language entailed in planning the actual performance, the children will be involved in retelling the story, sequencing the events and creating their own spoken lines, with or without a narrator. Characterisation of the voices provides scope for practising fluency, speed, volume, expression and intonation. Developing an understanding of the needs of an audience can also be a valuable product of working with puppets.

Masks

Many of the learning processes described in the previous section on puppets are also true of masks. The difference lies in the fact that a mask enables the child to use movement and gesture as well as voice. This is useful when children are role-playing within a particular situation but lack confidence. A mask can literally be a place to hide whilst exploring new language, thus adding an element of fun but also a feeling of safety. Masks can be used in free role-play and improvisation, and are also useful when children are presenting their work to others.

Mime

Mime can provide an active visual resource to accompany stories or explanations. It can also provide a framework for transferring thoughts, ideas or instructions into gesture. These approaches offer ways of supporting the language and learning of EAL pupils, from the use of mime both by the teacher and by the children themselves. There are various contexts within which mime might be used, for example:

■ during a story

- after a story
- when giving instructions for a task
- during an explanation
- as part of a question and answer session
- as an end-product to a piece of work
- when giving feedback.

When using mime for any of these purposes, it is also possible to vary the dynamic of the mime as follows:

- teacher instructs – child or children mime
- teacher mimes – child guesses
- pupils instruct each other to mime
- pupils plan and prepare a mime for others
- pupils read and mime cue cards for others to guess.

The mime might be used for short caption-type activities such as explaining vocabulary (e.g. prepositions, direction, speed), changing the meaning of same-phrase construction (e.g. 'She is cleaning her teeth. Now she is washing her face. Finally, she is drying her face.') and revisiting vocabulary (e.g. recapping on common occupations). The mime may take the form of short captions (words or phrases) for explanation, demonstration or guessing. Alternatively it may be presented in longer sequences to show to the rest of the group or class.

Drama and technology

There are many commercial products aimed at teaching languages through recorded training programmes – listening, repeating and checking all being important processes in the learning. However, these tend to be designed for individual use so have a limited role in the primary classroom situation. For short periods using headphones, language software can provide an additional supplement to practising and consolidating specific aspects of spoken language, and the more interactive software packages offer the added dimension of recording the learner's voice and giving automated feedback. This latter approach can be usefully hijacked by teachers by using drama to add interactivity to existing, and sometimes quite basic, technology!

Using audio-visual technology as part of drama with a partner or in a group can be productive and rewarding because it provides instant context and an additional resource for modelling. Listening to a short soundtrack together, or watching a focused clip of video that can be replayed, provides a stimulus or a framework for role-play. Popular television programmes and documentaries are particularly good for capturing children's interest in order to emulate language, for example presenting a short clip from *Blue Peter*, with props.

Teachers can create their own short sound recordings on a laptop for specific purposes and this takes very little time indeed. The purpose of the learning should be carefully considered in order to steer the dialogue towards a particular focus. For example, a conversation between a waiter/waitress and customer in a cafe might go something like this:

Waiter:	Good morning. Can I help you?
Customer:	Good morning. Please may I see the menu?
Waiter:	Yes, of course. Here you are.
Customer:	Hmmmm . . . Please may I have a cup of coffee and a cheese sandwich?
Waiter:	Brown bread or white bread?
Customer:	White please.
Waiter:	OK. Thank you.

Two children could replay the tape as often as they like, and play with the dialogue themselves in the role-play area, which would be set up as a cafe. Recording their own dialogue, and listening to check and compare, could be an additional part of the activity. Playing their final version to the teacher could provide evidence of their work. Developing the activity even further by introducing new vocabulary to order different things in the cafe would be an appropriate extension of their work.

Short extracts from television and film can provide a useful resource to stimulate interest and model language, particularly for older children. The key point when planning is to ensure that the objective for learning is clear and focused. Recording tailored dialogue can also help to support the reading of play scripts.

Talking tins represent the simplest form of sound technology but can be used very successfully in combination with drama to support EAL learners. Talking tins are small coloured disc devices onto which you can record a short message or phrase. They are very easy for even the youngest children to use, with clear buttons for recording and playing back. The length of the message depends on the model but ranges from eight seconds to 30 seconds. Teachers rather than children can record on to the tin, for example if there are particular words of phrases that need to be heard and learned as part of the drama, such as recording questions that have to be answered in role.

CHAPTER

9

Performance drama and theatre

Chapter overview

This chapter aims to provide you with a basic knowledge of the more technical aspects of theatre in performance. It discusses:

- moving from experience to performance

- the place of theatre arts in the primary curriculum

- expressive arts in the primary school

- cross-curricular creativity

- theatre skills and crafts

- working with theatre professionals

- developing critical responses

- a glossary of theatrical terms for children

- resources and professional development to support your teaching.

Moving from experience to performance

Chapter 1 describes the spectrum of drama in primary schools from experiential approaches that help children develop their personal thinking and understanding through to pure theatrical performance that is produced for the benefit of an audience. Much of what has been described in this book has been geared towards the former end of that spectrum. However, there will be times when you will need to provide children with opportunities to present their work in a more polished format: for example an assembly for parents and carers, a Christmas pantomime or an end-of-year production. This chapter provides more specialist information about the practicalities of theatrical performance. The benefits of this side of educational drama to children can be significant. Not only does performance drama enable children to build their confidence to express and present their work to others, it also offers opportunities to learn other skills that translate to other parts of the curriculum.

Expressive arts in the primary school

Drama, music, art and dance are sometimes referred to as the Performing Arts. However, in primary education it is more appropriate to use the term Expressive Arts, which encompasses a more integrated arts approach and also includes writing. Performance skills, although they have some part to play in young children's education, are quite subject-specific and specialist, whereas 'expressive' skills are more transferable and can be used for the exploration, development and communication of thoughts and ideas.

Children have an entitlement to a broad and balanced curriculum and more recently there has been wider recognition of the tremendous impact that creativity can have on the development of children's learning and well-being. The arts are part of life, and if the primary curriculum is to reflect a broad and balanced approach to life then it must, by default, include a comprehensive arts programme. The arts, on one level, are a source of enjoyment, challenge and recreation – a part of life that is separate from work (apart from for those who work in the arts industry). On another level, they are engines of cultural transmission: the transmission of stories, emotions, philosophies, ideas, belief systems and change that are part of the fabric of society itself. All children need to be given the opportunity to develop an awareness of the existence of the arts, an understanding of the ways in which they communicate their stories and messages, and an enjoyment of the sheer pleasures they have to offer. This in turn can provide them with the skills and aspirations to express their own ideas through different media, and to recognise their entitlement to understanding and enjoying arts activities and events beyond school. If children are denied access to all this because of a narrow, deficit curriculum, they are missing not only the chance to express themselves through such channels but also the means to enjoy, appreciate and learn from the work of others, now and in their future adult lives.

Theatre has always had a central social role to play in the lives of human beings, evidence of which goes right back to the Ancient Greeks. Apart from the period from 1642 to 1660 when the Puritans succeeded in closing down English theatres, there has been a strong tradition of theatre in Britain, always reflecting the moods and ideas of the times. Medieval Mystery Plays, Elizabethan travelling players performing Shakespeare, Restoration comedy, Victorian melodrama and later Victorian political drama all paved the way to the tapestry of theatrical genres available today: musical, farce, comedy, kitchen-sink drama, psycho-drama, political and social drama and others. Likewise, in other parts of the world there is a rich variety of theatre, from the tragicomedy of Chekhov in Russia to Aboriginal representations of the Dreamtime.

Of all the arts subjects, theatre arts lend themselves to the integration of arts subjects most naturally. In the primary school, the preparations and performance can include music, dance, art and design technology as a holistic part of the drama. This does not necessarily mean that the other arts subjects should always be driven by the drama, never standing alone in their own right – far from it. But it does mean that planning for performance drama in the primary school can provide golden opportunities for providing meaningful contexts for the other arts subjects. Indeed, it can also offer a highly creative vehicle for the exploration, delivery and presentation of other curriculum areas.

Cross-curricular creativity

It is a welcome sign that, following a significant number of years of a narrowly defined and restrictive approach to curriculum delivery, in particular of English, creativity is returning once more to primary schools. Research has proved time after time that children thrive and grow when their learning is structured within a well-planned framework that provides effective opportunities for creativity. Later on, creativity in the workplace promotes economic growth and encourages problem-solving, teamwork and solutions-focused attitudes. For primary children, not only does a creative curriculum motivate and engage, it can also help them to make connections and meaning between subjects more efficiently and effectively. Other subjects in the curriculum, including other arts subjects, can be used in conjunction with theatre arts in two ways: as curriculum content and as curriculum application.

Curriculum content

This approach is where the content matter of a curriculum area is used as all or part of the subject matter for the drama. Examples of this might include:

- English:
    a. KS1 – dramatisation of story into puppet theatre
    b. KS2 – working with extracts from Shakespeare
- Science:
    c. KS1 – dance-drama of the life cycle of plants
    d. KS2 – the environmental impact of disturbing the food chain
- History:
    e. KS1 – the life story of a famous character
    f. KS2 – myths and legends of Ancient Greece
- Geography:
    g. KS1 – a visit to a farm or a city
    h. KS2 – a town divided by opinion about a new motorway.

Curriculum application

This approach is where the skills from a curriculum area are applied generically to the overall planning, preparation and performance of the drama. Examples of this might include:

- Maths:
    i. KS1 – numbering, sorting or counting of tickets
    j. KS2 – calculating income from ticket sales/translating scales of designs
- Design and Technology:
    k. KS1 – designing, making and evaluating props
    l. KS2 – designing, making and evaluating models for sets and scenery
- Information and Communication Technology:
    m. KS1 – designing tickets or programmes
    n. KS2 – recording sound or visual projections
- Art:
    o. KS1 – graphic design of posters, after looking at the work of professionals
    p. KS2 – creating scenery from models, after looking at the work of professionals
- Music:
    q. KS1 – singing songs from memory, developing control of breathing, dynamics, rhythm and pitch
    r. KS2 – rehearsing and presenting pupil compositions
- Dance:
    s. KS1 – exploring moods and feelings, using rhythmic responses and contrasts of speed, shape, direction and level
    t. KS2 – creating simple characters and narratives.

All these examples relate directly to National Curriculum requirements for each subject. Not only do they illustrate the scope for using performance as a context for applying a range of skills, they also show how the National Curriculum can be planned creatively in ways that will motivate children by providing a purposeful context and, in doing so, help them learn more effectively.

Theatre skills and crafts

Never under-estimate children's motivation and enthusiasm to learn new skills, especially when they are connected with drama, film and television! You will usually find that the children are extremely keen to learn and try new techniques because they relate to popular culture and are fun to do. The application of skills and knowledge to the creation of performance can make a noticeable impact upon all those involved. Acknowledging and developing theatre skills and crafts in your work with children, where appropriate, is giving full respect to drama as an expressive art, and providing useful techniques that can enhance wider learning. However, it is important to achieve a balance. Over-emphasis on skills can become tedious if driven relentlessly and where not appropriate. On the other hand, lack of emphasis on skills can mean that children do not have the tools to create powerful drama for communication; this can lead to frustration and work that is of a poor quality. Learning objectives and goals should be clear, standards and expectations should be high, but so should the engagement and enjoyment.

Acting

Improvisation undoubtedly helps children to develop understanding of characters, and this can be a good way to prepare children for a part. Indeed, many professional directors put their actors through the paces of improvising different perspectives on a scene before moving into the scripted version. In school you might be using the improvisation as the stimulus for writing the script.

Here are some simple key starting points to guide you through the sorts of things you might encourage children to learn about acting.

- Movement affects the audience's perception of the character by creating visual images.
- Stillness can also be used for dramatic effect.
- The voice can be used in many different ways, and the expression tells part of the story.
- The voice needs to project so the audience can hear.
- Speaking too quickly will distort the sound. (Children tend to rush to get their bit over with! They will need practice in slowing down. Over-emphasising this can sometimes help.)
- Pauses can sometimes be as important and dramatic as speaking.
- Physical gesture (e.g. folding arms if on the defensive, scratching nose if nervous) can add to the drama.
- Props can be used to provide physical gestures (e.g. fiddling with an ornament at an awkward point).
- The relationships between the characters can be shown in speech, facial expressions and actions.
- Lines spoken are driven by a thought in the character's head (motivation).
- Characters should not look at the audience. It destroys the 'pretence', and also can distract the actor if they see someone they know! However, if they are narrating or the drama demands a direct address to engage the audience, then it is appropriate to look out there.

All these points can be differentiated according to the age of the children. It is up to you to adapt what you teach depending on the reasonable learning outcomes that can be expected for different groups of learners. For example, your interpretation of the first bullet point could range from 'If you are skipping on to the stage, the audience will see that you are happy. Skip on and try to show me how happy you are' to 'How can we show the audience by the way you move that you are sad as you walk across the stage?' The simple purpose of acting is to create believability for the audience, and that is the emphasis you should always place on skills development with children. In other words, they are taking part in building an artistic 'illusion', rather than training to become star idols!

Directing

The ways in which you direct children, if you are working towards a class performance for assembly or for a production, will significantly affect the development of their confidence. If you over-criticise them for making mistakes they will very likely become increasingly nervous about the whole thing. Make it enjoyable; don't be afraid to repeat things giving lots of encouragement each time, plus an additional focus for next time. Here are some simple guidelines.

- Be careful not to typecast children into roles that may reinforce sensitive issues.
- If you have to audition, treat this with sensitivity, ensuring that every child gets a part and is told about the positive things they have to offer to this part.
- Rehearse in small chunks to start with. These can be repeated in fun ways to help teach and consolidate, rather than doing too much, which the children then forget.
- Start to rehearse the full, continuous piece only when they are feeling confident with the shorter sections.
- Show that you value everyone, especially the small players. 'Guards, you stood really still during that scene, and you looked very stern. Well done. It's not easy to stand still for so long!'
- Make sure there are no idols or prima donnas!
- Explain and use technical language appropriate to the age (see the glossary at the end of this chapter). Children will enjoy acquiring this new vocabulary, and will do so quickly especially if they hear you repeating it often.
- Improvise small sections to help the children understand situations and characters.
- Give clear instructions about where and when to move.
- Weave in as many of the children's own ideas as you can. Help them to feel that it is their work. Always be open to suggestions.
- Don't be afraid to demonstrate!
- Make notes during rehearsals to feed back to individuals.
- Teach the children not to turn their back on the audience unless it is for dramatic effect.
- Stand at the back of the hall so they have to project their voices. If you sit at the front they will talk to the front.
- Tell them how their work makes you feel when appropriate.

Rehearsals

Rehearsals should be well planned to avoid children getting bored and the whole process becoming a chore. Several practical suggestions might help you here.

- If it is an extra-curricular production, provide a clear rehearsal timetable for every child. Rehearse different scenes on different days, with a list of who is required and when. Include the technical rehearsal and the dress rehearsal on the list so that good notice is given of your expectations.

- If it is part of your class work, it can still be good to provide a schedule. This also enables you to model writing for this purpose, encourages the children to read for information and helps you to plan the time needed. Again, a schedule sets out expectations, in particular of when lines need to be learned!

- Only rehearse for short periods, especially in KS1. Better to repeat a little several times and enable them to enjoy the praise of success than to practise a long stretch which they will not remember.

- Sub-contract sections to be rehearsed without you (e.g. small group of children with another adult, older children with a pupil director in the reading corner).

- Never ridicule mistakes. Correct supportively and demonstrate whenever appropriate. Praise specifics when they get it right.

Set design

Designing a set for a play provides opportunities for the development of art and technology skills, and sometimes maths. The stages of design can include:

- preliminary sketches
- floor plans
- models
- final construction.

The children can be involved at different levels, but it is clear that there is much scope for cross-curricular work here. Designing and interpreting floor plans, for instance, is a wonderfully practical and purposeful way of teaching mapping skills for geography. The first decision to be made is how to seat the audience. The traditional stage in front of rows of seating is not necessarily the only option. Figure 9.1 shows how an audience might be placed in one of three different positions.

Sets can be divided into two types. *Symbolic sets* are simple sets where things are just represented symbolically. *Realistic sets* are where you aim to create the illusion of reality, such as a room. Sets might be interior or exterior and you need to consider how scene changes will happen if appropriate. Clearly, scene design can only be discussed briefly here, but the following suggestions offer some practical advice:

- Different levels can create visual interest (Figure 9.2).
- Rostra do not always need to be parallel or at right angles to the audience.
- Walls and climbing bars can be disguised with fabric.
- Camouflage nets create wonderful effects, especially for forests.
- Try to use real furniture rather than dressing up school chairs and tables.

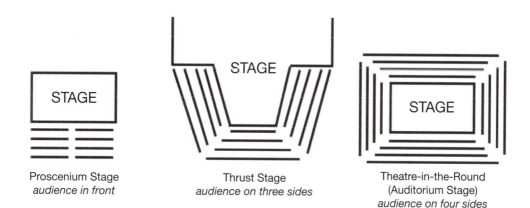

FIGURE 9.1 Placing the audience.

- Shops will usually help by lending furniture and props, especially if you acknowledge them in the programme.
- Parents and carers will also be a willing source, for artefacts and practical help.
- Screens can be useful to hide characters.
- Check to see if any scenery is casting shadows.
- Block off any view of backstage activities. The sight of children jumping up and down while waiting to go on is very distracting for the audience!
- It is, of course, important to carry out a thorough risk assessment on your set. Involving the children in this can be an excellent way of raising their own awareness of safety issues. Fire-proof materials, clear exits and trip hazards are obvious

Rostra can be used creatively to add visual interest.
Different levels and angles can help you achieve this.

FIGURE 9.2 Using levels and angles.

starting points, but identifying potential risks and minimising these by specified actions is the key process that will help you to spot other more unusual hazards.

Sound

Additional sound can be used for a variety of reasons as part of a performance, and there are different ways of achieving effects for different purposes. Sound production can be divided broadly into three categories:

1. *atmospheric sound* – to help create a mood, such as points of tension or humour, e.g. pathos music as Cinderella is left alone to scrub the floor

2. *functional sound* – which is almost like a prop to help the drama and create the illusion of reality, e.g. a telephone ringing

3. *sound markers* – to act as boundaries or signals, e.g. music at the end of the first half to signal the interval.

In school performances it is quite appropriate to use commercially produced sound, music and effects, with permission from the copyright holder (the BBC produces excellent CDs of sound effects from creaking doors to seaside beaches). Wherever possible, the children should be involved in the decision making, development and production of the sound. Clearly, there is an enormous amount of scope for composition and performance as required for the music curriculum. Older children could even take on the role of conductor during the performance. Other useful things to remember are:

- For live sound or the use of recordings, the children should follow a cue sheet that tells them when to play.
- Use good-quality speakers and place them where they won't dominate the actors' voices.
- Use the counter on your CD player or computer to mark the cues accurately.
- Make a backup recording.
- Have a technical rehearsal as well as a dress rehearsal.
- Keep a spare CD player or computer in reserve.
- Check the recording before a performance.
- Play appropriate music before the performance to set the mood – also during any interval and afterwards.

Lighting

Controlling the lighting in a production can make an enormous difference to the moods and atmospheres. Some schools are equipped with spotlights in the hall, but others have to hire lighting. If neither of these options is possible in your school, or if your performance is only a small-scale production (e.g. class assembly or a showing to another class), it is quite feasible to change the lighting in ways that will convince the children that they are doing something special and also create enhancing effects for the audience.

Home-made lighting effects

There is much you can create from resources you already have. Here are some practical examples:

- Use coloured gels (see next section) over the auditorium lights.
- Turn off the hall lights over the audience but not over the acting area.
- Use a redundant overhead projector (with or without gel) to direct a local pool of light.
- Project created or downloaded images from a computer onto a back wall or sheet.
- Direct desk lamps towards spots and move around if needed.
- Shine torches from the wings or by the actors themselves.
- Use coloured party light bulbs.
- Place table lamps strategically to create a different effect.
- Wire a household dimmer switch into a connector board to control lamps. This should be checked by a qualified electricitian.

Vary the lighting to mark a change of scene or mood (e.g. hall lights off/torches on). Sudden change can have an impact on the audience. Also, be sure to give recognition and status to the lighting technicians and provide them with clipboards and cue sheets. They should also be responsible for running checks before the performance.

Professional light hire

There are companies that hire out lighting equipment. Indeed, many theatres hire rather than buy their own lights, or hire additional specialised resources for specific productions. It is beyond the scope of this book to outline all you need to know about this particularly technical aspect of theatre. It is advisable to involve someone who knows something about lighting and electrics if you are new to stage lighting, or certainly read more specialised information. However, there are one or two basic principles which can be outlined here. For instance, every light casts a shadow. You therefore need to balance the lighting from all sides to eliminate unwanted shadows. Lights overhead cast different shadows on the actors' faces from lights shining upwards from the floor.

Stage lights are usually high voltage and get very hot indeed, so safety is a big issue. Suspended lights should always have a safety chain, and freestanding lights should always be weighted down and have a well-defined prohibited area all around them. Children should *never* be allowed close to freestanding spotlights. Connecting leads should always be taped to the floor.

One of the most useful pieces of equipment is a dimmer board. This has digital switches that will dim one light or a group of lights, depending on what you connect to it. The more advanced computerised dimmer boards can enable you to plan lighting changes digitally, so at the press of a switch one group of lights might go down while a different set comes up. If you are not hiring lights, you may still find it useful to visit a theatrical light hire company to buy gels. These are coloured celluloid sheets which can be cut to fit over lights to create a special effect. There are over 80 different colours available and they can be used singly or in combination to mix colours. Most useful are:

Straw	warm, sunny
Primary Red	sunsets, fire
Deep Blue	cold, water
Primary Green	forest
Pale Lavender	natural light
Pale Salmon	fairyland, rosy glow
Sky Blue	sky

Make-up

There are two main reasons for using stage make-up: first, to change the appearance of the actor (e.g. to make them look older); second, to counteract the draining effects of bright stage lights. If you are not using stage lighting, you should not need to use make-up unless it is to create characters. Masks are also a useful way of achieving this effect.

The use of make-up requires some knowledge of design and application. There are also important hygiene issues to be considered. Here are some simple pointers.

- Spot-check all children for allergic reactions before applying any significant quantity of make-up.
- Check for infectious skin conditions that might spread.
- Clean application sticks and sponges before using them on a new person.
- A towel around the neck and shoulders, and headband to hold back hair, are essential.
- A base of moisturiser or cold cream should always be applied before using stage make-up.
- Use the child's natural lines (e.g. for grumpy character, ask child to frown and follow their natural frown lines to apply the wrinkles).
- Dark shades create hollows and depth, light shades bring the face outwards; so, to make a nose appear thinner, apply shadows down each side and light make-up down the ridge.
- Eyebrows often need accentuating.
- Apply fixing-powder with cotton wool to prevent the stage paint from melting.
- Remove make-up with cold cream before trying to wash off.
- Wigs make a dramatic difference to appearance, even those which are home-made from wool or curled paper.

Box office

The making and selling of tickets for a performance offers golden opportunities for involving the children in useful learning tasks. The three advantages to this are:

- It gives them a sense of ownership and responsibility.
- It offers maths opportunities with a real-life context.
- It saves you having to do it!

Box office activities might include planning the size and design of the tickets (how many to a sheet of A4), planning the auditorium layout (how many chairs to a row, how many rows), numbering rows and tickets, calculating prices and selling tickets, giving change etc. Two box office managers could be selected each day, 10 minutes before the start of school, to sell tickets to parents and carers, keep a tally and total up the money. This could be simplified for younger children by getting them to keep a tally sheet, and ensuring that the ticket prices are simple, easy figures.

Publicity

Likewise, the design of posters, photographic displays for the 'foyer' and programmes can provide excellent learning activities. The programme in particular offers scope for different styles of writing (advertisements, actor profiles, synopsis, scene list etc.). As with all writing and art activities, it is important to show the children examples of professional posters and programmes before expecting them to embark upon their own ideas. Reproducing a programme that includes a piece of work from every child is a tremendous endorsement of purpose, and there is no doubt that the children will be thrilled to see the mass production and sale of their efforts!

Working with theatre professionals

As with many areas of work in the primary school, providing opportunities for children to meet and work with professionals and specialists can enrich the learning and engagement. Visits to see performances are one obvious starting point if you have a local theatre, and indeed it is stated clearly in the National Curriculum for English that this should happen. Many theatres have an education officer whose job it is to help you maximise the impact of theatre visits. It is not unreasonable to apply a school policy of one theatre trip per term for all classes. This enables you to plan for a wide range of performances, for example pantomime, dramatisation of children's literature, appropriate topical drama, puppet shows, mime, ballet, contemporary dance and so on. It is important to provide a variety of experiences; if children are only ever taken to pantomimes they are likely to develop a very limited perception of theatre. They need to experience a *range* of genres if they are to develop truly discerning skills of critical response. When taking children to a theatre, it is sometimes possible to arrange backstage tours, either in addition to seeing the performance or as a separate visit. This enables them to talk to a variety of people working in the theatre: wardrobe manager, stage technician, make-up artists, director, theatre manager, box office manager and so on, in addition to the actors. Both a performance and a tour require a certain level of preparation beforehand. The more the children know before the visit, the more they will be able to ask appropriate questions in order to extend their learning.

It is possible to bring the theatre into school. Most theatre-in-education (TIE) companies work 'on the road', performing and working with children in school-based workshops. These workshops can be with small groups, whole classes or even the whole school, and might involve exploring themes, explaining their work or developing new drama with the children. It is also worth remembering that many other organisations offer theatrical experiences, for example the National Trust, stately homes such as Warwick Castle and some museums. Similarly, it is possible to invite individual adults into school to talk about their work or to run workshops. Some puppeteers, for instance, will put on a performance, followed by a practical workshop on making puppets. Mime artists are also available to demonstrate and collaborate. You may wish to invite in an actor or designer to talk about his or her work and answer the children's questions. There is a growing number of arts organisations that will facilitate the work of professionals in schools, most notably the highly successful Creative Partnerships project, which has had a hugely positive impact on the creative development of schools across the UK. The Learning through Action Trust is another effective organisation that works practically with children (and runs courses for teachers) both in schools and from its base in Berkshire. It provides experiential workshops on topics from different subject areas, and also specialises in working with children who have behavioural difficulties. A list of contact details for these and other useful organisations is provided in Appendix 2.

Developing critical responses

The Programmes of Study for Drama, published by the Arts Council in 2003 in a booklet called *Drama in Schools (Second Edition)*, outline three areas of assessment in the End of Key Stage Statements: Making, Performing and Responding. (The full Programmes of Study for Key Stages 1 and 2 can be found in Appendix 3 of this book, and are discussed in more detail in Chapter 10.) Responding to drama, both that of others and also their own, is an important part of children's learning and development. The requirement to respond focuses their observations, and the requirement to communicate those responses involves the organisation and externalisation of thoughts and ideas. Watching a play may be an enjoyable experience, but going on to reflect upon and discuss that experience helps to develop skills of oracy and literary analysis, both important parts of the English curriculum.

Pupils' evaluations of and reflections on their own performances in school is a valuable part of their ongoing development and progression. They are also an essential component of assessment for learning. Evaluating professional theatrical performances is a valuable process because the art form provides such a tremendous variety of dynamics to which children can respond: different actors, characters, costumes, set design, scenery changes, music, lighting, sound effects and audience reaction. The provision of all this material at a professional level can raise children's aspirations of what is possible and help them to develop a language of response that they can also use when talking about their own work.

There are five broad types of response that can encompass a range of subjects. Examples are given below for each key stage, but you should recognise that the range within each type of response is enormous. 'Giving an opinion', for instance, could be about the way the play ends, a particular actor's performance, the choice of music and so on. The categorisation of these response types is simply intended as a starting point to raise awareness of the possibilities.

- Giving an opinion
  a. KS1 – describing a part that they did or did not enjoy
  b. KS2 – agreeing/disagreeing with a character portrayal
- Justifying opinion
  c. KS1 – saying why they did not like a certain character
  d. KS2 – giving examples of contradictory character behaviour
- Drawing comparisons
  e. KS1 – comparing a character's behaviour with a real-life example
  f. KS2 – comparing a stage production with a book of the same
- Offering alternatives
  g. KS1 – suggesting different ideas for costume designs
  h. KS2 – suggesting alternative interpretations of text
- Empathising
  i. KS1 – describing how a character might have felt at a certain point
  j. KS2 – describing character motivation for a particular action

To elicit such responses and nurture an ethos in which children feel empowered to express their own opinions and feel confident to back this up with evidence or reasoned argument, the teacher's role needs to be one of encouragement. It also needs skilled open questioning that leads children to respond analytically rather than closed questions that encourage jumping through hoops to come up with the correct answer! Questions should be open-ended, and should focus on a range of criteria. For example, 'Did you like that play?' limits the possible responses to 'Yes' or 'No', whereas 'What did you like about that play?' broadens the scope. 'What did you think about the sound effects they used?' focuses the reflection into a particular area, which is a necessary part of extending the children's considerations.

Glossary of theatrical terms

Children love to use new words, and words that relate to theatre, film and television can be particularly appealing. At one level, there is a feeling of glamour and 'grown-upness' about such special terminology which intrigues and motivates children. But, more importantly, modelling the language and encouraging them to follow your example plays an important part in extending their vocabulary, learning about language use and increasing their knowledge and understanding of the art form. The following theatrical terms are ones that children should be able to learn and use. You will probably be familiar with many of them already, but the list is intended as a reminder to you to use them.

actor:	person who performs dramatic roles for an audience, term now commonly used for male and female
audition:	a test reading from a script or improvisation to help the director choose the right person for each part
auditorium:	the area of the theatre where the audience sits
blocking:	planning the moves for a scene
box office:	place from which tickets are sold
cast:	the full set of actors in the play
costume:	specially designed clothes for the actor to wear
critic:	person who is paid to watch a play then write a review for a newspaper or magazine
dimmer board:	electrical board of dimmer switches, each of which controls a light or group of lights
director:	person who plans how the play will be performed and instructs the actors at rehearsals
down-stage:	the front of the stage nearest to the audience
dress rehearsal:	final rehearsal in costume
front of house:	areas in front of the stage (auditorium, box office, foyer etc.)
gels:	coloured filters that are put in front of lights to create special effects
house lights:	the non-stage lights in the auditorium
props:	short for 'properties'; items additional to scenery and costumes which the actors need for their performance
standby!:	an instruction to members of the cast or technical team to be ready to take action
stage hand:	assistant who helps to change scenery
stage left:	the area of the stage to the actor's left when facing the audience
stage right:	the area of the stage to the actor's right when facing the audience
strike the set:	take down the set once the play is finished
tabs:	the curtains
technical rehearsal:	penultimate rehearsal to add lighting and sound
up-stage:	the back of the stage furthest away from the audience
wings:	each side of the stage where the actors wait to come on

Resources and professional development to support your teaching

Extending your professional knowledge of theatre can help you feel more confident and further stimulate your own enthusiasm and creativity. There is much for teachers to enjoy in this area of work with children, and there is a wealth of support available in the way of information, guidance, enrichment and continuing professional development. Film Education is a charity funded by the UK film industry that will send you superb teacher guidance and activities for children linked to films – and many of these are free! The Royal Shakespeare Company (RSC) Education Department produces good information packs, resources for schools and professional development for teachers of all key stages including the Early Years Foundation Stage. Other types of resources available from theatres for teachers can also be used in the classroom. Used tickets, programmes, posters, set design plans, costume drawings and photographs can usually be obtained if you build up a good contact with your nearest theatre. These are enormously useful for children to look at and discuss when they are working on their own designs. Information and resource packs are also available from many theatres, particularly larger theatres that have Arts Council funding for that purpose. Funding is also used to sponsor special projects in schools such as Theatre in Residence. It is surprising how much free information and resource material is available if you only know where to look! The list of contact details in Appendix 2 offers further suggestions to help you.

Drama and assessment

Chapter overview

This chapter aims to help you understand how the drama components within English can be assessed. It also looks at the wider issues of assessment, and how important they can be in informing your planning for high-quality children's learning. In particular, it discusses:

- assessment to support learning

- differentiation

- the wider scope of assessing through drama

- the key characteristics of good assessment practice

- a framework for assessing English curriculum drama

- a whole-school approach to assessing drama.

Assessment to support learning

Assessment appears in many guises in primary education but they are all inextricably linked to the quality of the learning. Lesson planning should be linked to ongoing assessments of children's learning so that activities consolidate previous acquisition and extend it further at every level. Oral and written feedback should ensure that children know how well they are doing, or what they need to work on differently in order to improve. However, only if it is based on accurate assessment can providing children with clear steps for improvement be effective. Sometimes this might take place during the lesson through observation, particularly in drama, when teachers can intervene and support actively throughout the lesson. Effective questioning is another means of doing this. Encouraging children of all ages to evaluate their own work is also an extremely powerful means of moving the learning forward. Research shows that where children have ownership of an improvement agenda they are more motivated to apply it.

Differentiation

At the heart of good teaching lies effective planning of activities that move every child forward from their current understanding and skills to the next stage. The ideal model is one in which this happens every day through consistent and secure steps forward. Simply providing a class of children with a 'one-size-fits-all' lesson will usually result in some finding it too difficult, some finding it too easy and some finding it just right, but, where learning is differentiated to meet the needs of different abilities, every child will be suitably challenged and make good progress. Most of the practical examples provided in this book have been about the mechanisms of the drama. When using the drama to teach specific skills of English it is important to include differentiated learning objectives so that it is clear how you will be moving the children forward at different levels. In Chapter 1 the four roles of drama were described and Table 1.1 provided three examples of how each might be used to promote language skills. Those examples have been developed in Table 10.1 to show how, although the drama technique might be the same for the class, the actual learning objectives could vary according to ability.

Although the activity might be planned around the drama, the actual learning might relate to an aspect of English. This demonstrates why the actual learning objectives should be made clear to the children and discussed throughout the activity. When

TABLE 10.1 Differentiated learning objectives for oracy, reading and writing

LANGUAGE FOCUS USING DRAMA	LOWER-LEVEL OBJECTIVE	MIDDLE-LEVEL OBJECTIVE	HIGHER-LEVEL OBJECTIVE
Oracy: using specific type of speaking in role Drama technique: dynamic duos where a teacher is interviewing a parent about a bullying incident	To listen to questions and respond appropriately	To ask appropriate questions	To ask questions that build on what the other person has said
Reading: interpreting scripts Drama technique: reading, planning and performing	To interpret the meaning	To read fluently and accurately	To develop interpretations of characters and events
Writing: recording an interview in role Drama technique: follow-up to the oracy example above	To record the key points in simple sentences, remembering all full stops and capital letters	To show logical sequencing of the main points and some question marks	To write more complex sentences with punctuation within them

planning, you need to be clear about the difference between what they will *do* and what they will *learn*.

The wider scope of assessing through drama

Assessment during drama can include a wide range of competencies such as performance skills, planning and creating, teamwork, problem solving and collaboration. This book focuses specifically on the aspects of drama that are included within the English curriculum, and a simple framework for assessing this is provided at the end of this chapter. But don't forget that drama can also provide extremely appropriate opportunities for assessing speaking and listening within the curriculum for English, as shown in Chapter 5. Likewise, many of the reading and writing activities described in Chapters 6 and 7 can provide useful contexts and evidence for assessing literacy skills as shown in the previous section. If children are to gain the maximum benefits of learning English through drama you need to plan with a sound understanding of what you expect them to achieve. Effective planning works hand in hand with teacher expectations and assessment, so let us begin by looking at the key characteristics of good assessment practice.

Key characteristics of good assessment practice

The most effective types of assessment are those that are useful and move the learning forward. In particular, good assessment information should inform you and the child about what they can achieve competently and the progress that has been made. You should also be able to glean important information about the effectiveness of your teaching approach and where the learning needs to go next. The traditional forms of assessment are marking and testing. Sometimes this will be formative (ongoing) and sometimes it will be summative to benchmark a point reached at a certain time. However, all the benefits listed above can also happen when the assessment is taking place as an integral part of teaching and learning, rather than just an additional component at the end of the activity, because there can be more interaction between you and the children.

Integrating teaching, learning and assessment

Interaction means that instruction and feedback can be given as an ongoing part of the teaching, and children can respond accordingly. An integrated approach to assessment also means that the process can be assessed in addition to the product, and this is crucial if the teacher is to understand the full learning picture. Just as a piece of beautiful handwriting could belie a laborious process during which the pencil was held inappropriately and the letters formed from right to left, so a piece of thought-provoking and well-constructed drama might be the result of one dominant leader in a dysfunctional group rather than a collaborative effort. In both these examples, the teacher could make a glowing summative assessment of the end-product without being aware of the inadequate quality of the processes which were involved in their production.

Integrating assessment into everyday classroom activities encourages a reflective approach to teaching and learning and provides multi-faceted information which feeds into the educational process. This information might be from the child to you (e.g. answering a question), from you to the child (e.g. recapping on a point which has been misunderstood), from child to child (e.g. giving feedback) or self-evaluation (e.g. child reflecting on her own outcomes).

Clarity about what is assessed

Another feature of good assessment is a clear understanding by you and the children of what is being assessed. Your expectations should be made clear to children so that they know what they are aiming for, and can recognise their achievements. During a drama activity, which on the surface may appear to be an 'informal' learning situation, it is arguably even more important to make explicit to children what is required of them. So comments such as:

■ 'I shall be watching you all to see how carefully you are listening to each other.'

■ 'It is important to get the sequence of events in the right order. I shall be asking the other children to comment on that when you show your story later.'

■ 'The audience will need to hear you from the back of the hall, so I am going to stand there now to check if you are using your voices clearly and loudly, but without shouting.'

■ 'When you've finished playing in the home area, I want you to tell me about what your characters have been reading and writing.'

. . . all help the children to focus on the relevant learning points.

Useful evidence

Such clarity of purpose is also important when collecting evidence of children's progress. When conducting more summative forms of assessment, you need to be clear about how you will search the material to identify learning outcomes. So, with a scripted play written from an improvisation exercise, for example, you might be asking yourself any of the following questions:

■ Have they used language that is appropriate to the situation?

■ Have they provided implicit information in the dialogue?

■ Have they included additional information to develop characters?

■ Have they constructed a plausible ending during the sequence, as opposed to 'quickly finishing off' for convenience?

Asking yourself questions that can be clearly answered 'yes' or 'no', or with direct examples, is a helpful way to structure an assessment framework, and provides a more rigorous evaluation process than generalised statements such as 'They presented a good improvisation.'

Another point to remember about the nature of summative evidence is that it can tell you something useful only if it can be compared with other evidence from a different phase. In other words, it needs to be part of a fuller picture that provides evidence of progression.

Progression and change

Progression in learning means that something changes for the better: new knowledge is there, where it didn't exist before; a skill has appeared or improved; a concept has been acquired, can be explained. Skills are easier to measure than knowledge and concepts because they are observable whereas knowledge and concepts can only be observed within the contexts where they are being applied.

Seeing progression as evidence of change highlights the need to avoid deficit models of assessment which just identify 'gaps'. Gaps in a child's knowledge or competencies are useful only if they are considered within the context of a developmental continuum. In other words, if a gap coincides with the next stage of learning, then it is appropriate for it to be addressed. However, if it is too far along the sequential line of conceptual development it is usually more effective to provide other prerequisites for learning which are needed before the gap can be addressed.

Creating useful records

Good assessment requires record keeping that is systematic, easy to interpret, relevant and useful. Record keeping can take many forms, some being the child's own documentary evidence and others being your own. The drama process might involve any of the following types of records:

- diary of theatre visits (ongoing from Year 1 to 6)
- audio recordings of dialogue
- video evidence
- self-evaluation forms
- written work relating to drama context (e.g. news report)
- skills tick lists.

Giving status to the learning

When children are worried about being tested, it is usually because they believe it to be so important that they will in some way be in trouble if they 'fail'. At the other extreme drama is sometimes considered a 'soft' subject associated with leisure and pleasure. If drama is to be valued and respected by children, it is important that they recognise the place of assessment and the expectations that their teacher has within that framework. They also need to recognise that what they are doing is relevant to them personally. This can usually be achieved by making it explicit to the children that they are learning many useful skills in drama, by demonstrating that you are taking note of their learning and, perhaps most importantly, by giving them regular feedback on their progress.

A framework for assessing English curriculum drama

As explained in Chapter 4, the National Curriculum outlines a basic expectation for drama within speaking and listening.

At KS1, to participate in a range of drama activities, pupils should be taught to:

1. use language and actions to explore and convey situations, characters and emotions

2. create and sustain roles individually and when working with others

3. comment constructively on drama they have watched or in which they have taken part.

At KS2 they should be taught to:

4. create, adapt and sustain different roles, individually and in groups

5. use character, action and narrative to convey story, themes, emotions, ideas in plays they devise and script

6. use dramatic techniques to explore characters and issues (for example hot seating, flashback)

7. evaluate how they and others have contributed to the overall effectiveness of performances.

Table 10.2 illustrates how these requirements can be grouped into three areas, and assessed progressively. A photocopiable version is provided in Appendix 3 for your use.

This framework also includes, implicitly, the ways in which children work, independently and collaboratively. If we are concerned about whether children stay on task, can work towards targets, work with the ideas of others, can organise their work, plan tasks and material, set about solving problems and so on, then we need to observe and encourage them as they work to ensure that they are progressing in the right direction. Clearly, these skills can be assessed in many, if not all, subject areas, but drama is a particularly good place to do this systematically because collaborative skills have such a central part to play and are transferable across the curriculum. They also play an important part in developing life skills for children's future work and well-being. Don't be a slave to a framework such as this; follow your professional judgement to use it flexibly. Here is some further guidance on each of the three aspects.

Interpreting character

Interpreting character requires imagination and creativity. It can involve voice, action and expression. It also requires children to apply their imagination. When we try to define the word 'imagination' it is tempting to think about creating something from nothing. But that can never be true. Our imagination draws upon our experience. It takes events from our memory, things we have seen, heard, read, discussed, smelt, felt

TABLE 10.2 Framework for assessing the drama in English

INTERPRETING CHARACTER	PRESENTING	EVALUATING
Can introduce characters from stories into role-play	Can use language and actions to recreate a story in the role-play area or within a small group	Can talk about at least two different things that they liked or disliked about drama they have watched, and say why
Is confident to explore different characters through the use of voice and movement	Can present a mime or puppet performance to the class	Can discuss at least one constructive idea for improvement of drama they have watched
Can explore and talk about character motivation in different situations	Can interpret scripts and transform into performance	Can evaluate their own work in drama against the learning objective
Can create and sustain the role of a character, including the portrayal of emotions, when working with others	Can develop own ideas and construct into a format suitable for a selected audience	Can evaluate the impact of their contribution to drama work and talk about how they might improve it
Can use characterisation when interpreting scripts	Can transfer style elements from professional performances into their own work	Can evaluate how their work in drama has improved over time

and touched, both directly and indirectly (through the representations of others), and recreates them into new forms. Use of imagination, therefore, is about transferring knowledge and experience from one form into another. The richer the experiences provided for children, the more fertile their imaginations will be. Interpreting involves extracting meaning in order to make sense from one or more perspectives. The framework provides a progressive approach to this, starting with practical exploration of character (e.g. movement and speech), moving towards considering more complex features such as character motivation and thought, and then applying analytical skills to interpret more abstract characters through written texts. Understanding characters, whether it be from the perspective of a writer in role or the consideration of how a person might move, is an essential part of drama as experience and theatre as performance. Understanding the needs of an audience can also cover a range of levels; for example, writing in role involves selecting an appropriate genre for the intended reader, and portraying the movement of a character is helping the audience to understand and believe in that character.

Presenting

This is a generic aspect that is transferable across many areas of children's work in primary schools. The assessment of performance includes some integration of English skills. However, this aspect also offers opportunities to move into more specialist areas of drama and theatre arts. For example, assessing a child's voice projection and expression during an assembly for parents and carers will address the speaking and listening requirements, but could also be considered to be part of performance.

Evaluating

Developing evaluative skills is an essential aspect of children's education and is appropriate in other areas of the curriculum. For example: recognising how sounds can be used in different ways for effect in a particular scene links directly to music; using photographs from the past to create tableaux involves interpretation in history; and evaluating the accuracy of a reporter's 'television piece' about the effects of a volcanic eruption relates appropriately to geography. The drama requirements in the English curriculum focus on evaluation leading to more constructive analysis and criticism of children's own drama work and that of others. But don't forget that the more specific learning objectives relating to basic English skills as shown in Table 10.1 can also be strengthened through self- and peer assessment by the children themselves.

Progression: a whole-school approach

As with the assessment of all areas of learning, it is important to relate your assessments to progression. If assessment exists within a vacuum, unrelated to what has been achieved in the past and disconnected from what is planned for the next learning stages, then its value is questionable. No matter how excellent a teacher might be within the confines of their own classroom, a whole-school approach, where staff work as a team and where progression is monitored along commonly agreed continua, creates the optimum impact on children's learning. A whole-school approach to drama requires helpful guidance on how children might be expected to make progress during their seven years in school. This, combined with vertical planning of drama teaching methods, can result in a balanced approach which develops fully the potential of drama in the creative arts, in English and in other subject areas.

The levels provided in the previous framework are not necessarily intended to run parallel to National Curriculum levels. They are, however, intended to provide a starting point to help you focus on continuous development. You may wish to replace some of the prescribed competencies with others of your choice that you feel to be more appropriate to the children in your school. The important thing to remember is that an assessment framework should not drive you in directions that are unproductive or even impossible; it should assist you in providing what is best for the children, and this will almost always involve an amount of adaptation and development.

Further reading

Cave, S. (2006) *100+ Fun Ideas for Learning a Modern Foreign Language in the Primary Classroom: Activities for Developing Oracy and Literacy Skills*. Dunstable: Brilliant Publications.
A tried and tested collection of oracy and literacy activities to promote language learning.

Clipson-Boyles, S. (2010) *Supporting Language and Literacy 0–5*. London: Routledge.
This is a practical guide for the Early Years Foundation Stage. It provides clear, practical guidance underpinned by relevant theoretical frameworks and supported with photocopiable activities for training.

Doona, J. (2010) *A Practical Guide to Shakespeare for the Primary Classroom: 50 Schemes of Work and Lesson Plans*. London: Routledge.
This is an invaluable resource for introducing and developing work on Shakespeare with primary children.

Heathcote, D. and Bolton, G. (1996) *Drama for Learning*. Portsmouth, NH: Heinemann.
This seminal work is still in print and continues to provide a useful and inspiring background to the power of drama as a learning process.

Kerry, T. (ed.) (2010) *Cross-Curricular Teaching in the Primary School*. London: Routledge.
This book supports the learning benefits of integrated learning across the curriculum by demonstrating creative planning for maximum impact.

National Drama Publications
In addition to the twice-yearly magazine, National Drama also provides useful publications on focus issues (e.g. *Community Cohesion*, *Gifted and Talented Pupils*), many of which are downloadable at no cost. See Appendix 2 for contact details.

Palmer, S. (2010) *Speaking Frames: How to Teach Talk for Writing*. Abingdon: Taylor & Francis Group.
This covers ideas for children aged 8–10 and is an extremely useful book of ideas to promote writing through the dynamics of oracy. Supported by the underpinning theory and photocopiable resources.

Sellman, E. (2011) *Creative Learning to Meet Special Needs*. London: Routledge.
This books explains the importance of a creative approach to teaching in Key Stages 2 and

3, including personalised learning and interactive tasks in relation to pupils with special educational needs.

Theodorou, M. (2009) *Classroom Gems: Games, Ideas and Activities for Primary Drama.* Harlow: Pearson Publishing.
This is a useful practical book packed with ideas and lessons to try in the classroom and hall.

Thorp, G. (2005) *The Power of Puppets: Stories and Practical Ideas to Share with KS1 and KS2.* Trowbridge: Positive Press Ltd.
The title says it all! A useful practical resource.

Wagner, B.J. (1998) *Educational Drama and Language Arts: What Research Shows.* Portsmouth, NH: Heinemann.
A unique collection of research providing a compelling background to the evidence and supporting theories for the impact of drama on learning.

Useful organisations

Arts Council England
14 Great Peter Street, London, SW1P 3NQ
Tel: 0845 300 6200
Website: www.artscouncil.org.uk

Arts Council of Northern Ireland
MacNeice House, 77 Malone Road, Belfast, County Antrim, BT9 6AQ
Tel: 028 9038 5200
Website: www.artscouncil-ni.org

Arts Council of Wales
Bute Place, Cardiff, CF10 5AL
Tel: 0845 8734 900
Website: www.artswales.org.uk

Creative Partnerships
Great North House, Sandyford Road, Newcastle upon Tyne, NE1 8ND
Tel: 0844 811 2145
Website: www.creative-partnerships.com

Foundation for Community Dance
LCB Depot, 31 Rutland Street, Leicester, LE1 1RE
Tel: 0116 253 3453
Website: www.communitydance.org.uk

Film Education
91 Berwick Street, London, W1F 0BP
Tel: 020 7292 7330
Website: www.filmeducation.org

Learning through Action Trust
The LTA Centre, High Close School, Wiltshire Road, Wokingham, RG40 1TT
Tel: 0870 770 7985
Website: www.learning-through-action.org.uk

NALDIC (for EAL)
Building L46, University of Reading, London Road, Reading, RG1 5AQ
Tel: 0118 986 9040
Website: www.naldic.org.uk

National Drama
West Barn, Church Farm, Happisburgh, Norwich, NR12 0QY
Telephone: 0782 5776898
Website: www.nationaldrama.org.uk

National Literacy Trust
68 South Lambeth Road, London, SW8 1RL
Tel: 020 7820 6267
Website: www.literacytrust.org.uk

National Museum of the Performing Arts
Russell Street, London, WC2E 7PR
Tel: 020 7836 7891/2330

Puppet Centre Trust
Puppet Centre Trust, Battersea Arts Centre, Lavender Hill, Battersea, London,
SW11 5TN
Tel: 020 7228 533
Website: www.puppetcentre.org.uk

Royal Shakespeare Company
The Courtyard Theatre, Southern Lane, Stratford-upon-Avon, CV37 6BB
Tel: 0844 800 1110
Website: www.rsc.org.uk

Scottish Arts Council
12 Manor Place, Edinburgh, EH3 7DD
Tel: 0131 226 6051
Website: www.scottisharts.org.uk

The Society for Storytelling
The Morgan Library, Aston Street, Wem, Shropshire, SY4 5AU
Tel: 07534 578 386
Website: www.sfs.org.uk

The Theatre and Performance Museum Collection
V&A South Kensington, Cromwell Road, London, SW7 2RL
Tel: 020 7942 2000
Website: www.vam.ac.uk

Photocopiable resources

Child's Name:

	INTERPRETING CHARACTER	PRESENTING	EVALUATING
Level 1	Can introduce characters from stories into role-play	Can use language and actions to recreate a story in the role-play area or within a small group	Can talk about at least two different things that they liked or disliked about drama they have watched, and say why
Comments			
Level 2	Is confident to explore different characters through the use of voice and movement	Can present a mime or puppet performance to the class	Can discuss at least one constructive idea for improvement of drama they have watched
Comments			
Level 3	Can explore and talk about character motivation in different situations	Can interpret scripts and transform into performance	Can evaluate their own work in drama against the learning objective
Comments			
Level 4	Can create and sustain the role of a character, including the portrayal of emotions, when working with others	Can develop own ideas and construct into a format suitable for a selected audience	Can evaluate the impact of their contribution to drama work and talk about how they might improve it
Comments			
Level 5	Can use characterisation when interpreting scripts	Can transfer style elements from professional performances into their own work	Can evaluate how their work in drama has improved over time
Comments			

Record of professional drama experiences (theatre visits and visitors):

Year 1   Year 2

Year 3   Year 4

Year 5   Year 6

My theatre visits log

Name:

DATE	THEATRE	PLAY	SCORE OUT OF 10

My trip to the theatre

My name is

Here is my favourite character.

Here are some of the other characters.

This is the scenery.

I liked this play because

My visit to the theatre to see

My name is

My favourite character was

My favourite part was when

because

Theatre Review: L2

A theatre review of . . .

By theatre critic . . .

On

I went to the theatre.

The play was called

It was about

My favourite character was

because

I didn't like

because

The best part of the play was when

Theatre Review: L3

Theatre review of:

by

My first impression of this play was

Particularly good performances were given by

However,

was the least strong performance because

The set design was

One weakness of the production was

However, a real strength of this production was

I think it could have been even better if

Recommendation   out of 10

Telephone Message

To:
_____

From:
_____

Time:
_____

Message:
_____

_____

_____

Telephone Message

To:
_____

From:
_____

Time:
_____

Message:
_____

_____

_____

MENU

PRICE

SNACKS

MEALS

DESSERTS

DRINKS

References

Arts Council England (1992) *Drama in Schools*. London: Arts Council England.

Arts Council England (2003) *Drama in Schools (Second Edition)*. London: Arts Council England.

Berk, L.E. (1994) 'Why Children Talk to Themselves'. *Scientific American*, November, pp. 78–83.

Bercow, J. (2008) *The Bercow Report*. Nottingham: DCSF.

Bolton, G. (1979) *Towards a Theory of Drama in Education*. Harlow: Longman.

Brecht, B. (2007) *The Caucasian Chalk Circle*. London: Penguin Modern Classics.

Browne, A. (1994) *Zoo*. London: Red Fox Picture Books.

Browne, A. (2008) *Gorilla*. London: Walker.

Bruner, J. (1986) *Actual Minds, Possible Worlds*. Cambridge, MA: Harvard University Press.

Burningham, J. (1994) *Would You Rather . . .* London: Red Fox Picture Books.

Clay, M. (1979) *The Early Detection of Reading Difficulties*. London: Heinemann.

Clipson-Boyles, S.B. (1996) 'Teaching Reading through Drama', in Reid, D. and Bentley, D. (eds), *Reading On! Developing Reading at Key Stage 2*. Leamington Spa: Scholastic.

Clipson-Boyles, S. (2010) *Supporting Language and Literacy 0–5*. London: Routledge.

Collier, V. (1996) 'A Synthesis of Studies Examining Long-Term Language Minority Student Data'. *Bilingual Research Journal*, 16, pp. 187–212.

DES (1989) *National Curriculum Orders for English*. London: HMSO.

DfEE (1998) *The National Literacy Strategy: Framework for Teaching*. London: HMSO.

Education Reform Act (1988). London: HMSO.

EDWA (1997) *A Continuum in Writing (First Steps)*. East Perth: Education Department of Western Australia.

Frank, L. (1992) 'Writing to Be Read: Young Writers' Ability to Demonstrate Audience Awareness when Evaluated by Their Teachers'. *Research in Teaching English*, 26, pp. 132–155.

Hart, B. and Risley, T. (2003) 'The Early Catastrophe: The 30 Million Word Gap'. *American Educator*, 27 (1), pp. 4–9.

Hester, H. (1990) *Patterns of Learning*. London: CLPE.

HMI (1990) *The Teaching and Learning of Drama*. London: HMSO.

Hodgson Burnett, F. (2007) *The Secret Garden*. London: Penguin Modern Classics.

Hughes, T. (1993) *The Iron Woman*. London: Faber and Faber.

Hutchins, P. (1970) *Rosie's Walk*. London: Picture Puffins.

Kay, J. (1994) 'Duncan Gets Expelled', in *Two's Company*. London: Penguin.

King, C. (2003) *Stig of the Dump: New Edition*. London: Puffin Modern Classics.

NALDIC (2009) *Developing a Bilingual Pedagogy for UK Schools*. Reading: NALDIC.

NCC (1991) *Drama in the National Curriculum* (poster). London: HMSO.

Piaget, J. (1952) *The Origins of Intelligence in Children*. Madison, CT: International Universities Press.

Raison, G. (for the Education Department, Western Australia) (1994) *Writing: Developmental Continuum*. Melbourne: Longman.

Rose, J. (2009) *Independent Review of the Primary Curriculum*. Nottingham: DCSF.

Slade, P. (1958) *An Introduction to Child Drama*. London: University of London Press.

Stanovich, K. (1980) 'Towards an Interactive Compensatory Model of Differences in the Development of Reading Fluency'. *Reading Research*, 16, pp. 32–71.

QCA (1999) *The National Curriculum for England: English*. London: HMSO.

Vygotsky, L.S. (1978) *Mind in Society*. Cambridge, MA: Harvard University Press.

Wagner, J. (1999) *Dorothy Heathcote: Drama as a Learning Medium*. Portland, ME: Calendar Islands Publishers.

Way, B. (1967) *Development through Drama*. London: Longman.

Wells, G. (1986) *The Meaning Makers*. London: Hodder and Stoughton.

Index